RAISING
TRUMP

RAISING
TRUMP

IVANA TRUMP

GALLERY BOOKS

NEW YORK   LONDON   TORONTO   SYDNEY   NEW DELHI

G

Gallery Books
An Imprint of Simon & Schuster, Inc.
1230 Avenue of the Americas
New York, NY 10020

First Gallery Books hardcover edition September 2017

GALLERY BOOKS and colophon are registered
trademarks of Simon & Schuster, Inc.

For information about special discounts for bulk purchases,
please contact Simon & Schuster Special Sales at
1-866-506-1949 or business@simonandschuster.com.

The Simon & Schuster Speakers Bureau can bring authors to your live event.
For more information or to book an event, contact the Simon & Schuster Speakers
Bureau at 1-866-248-3049 or visit our website at www.simonspeakers.com.

Interior design by Jaime Putorti

Manufactured in the United States of America

10 9 8 7 6 5 4 3 2 1

Library of Congress Cataloging-in-Publication Data is available.

ISBN 978-1-5011-7728-6
ISBN 978-1-5011-7730-9 (ebook)

Insert 1, page 2, top left photo by Jiri Birch.
All other photos courtesy of Ivana Trump.

To my three amazing kids, Don, Ivanka,
and Eric, for making my life so full and fun.

To my parents, Babi and Dedo, and my
grandparents, for giving me all the love in the world.

To Trudy, Bridget, and Dorothy, for helping me every step of the way.

To David Moya, for taking care of me, my mother,
and my children in my house in Palm Beach.

And to Donald, the kids' father and my dear friend.

CONTENTS

INTRODUCTION

Nothing is worse than bratty, spoiled rich kids, right? You just want to rip the silver spoon right out of their mouths. Off the top of your head, you can probably think of a few adult children of the superrich who've thrown tantrums on airplanes, been arrested for drunk driving, made a sex tape, and wasted every advantage they've been given.

My three children—Donald Jr., Ivanka, and Eric—are the opposite. While campaigning for their father last year, they were praised for their intelligence, poise, dedication, and confidence. Many Americans formed their first impressions of my kids at the Republican National Convention in July 2016, where they gave speeches to support their father's campaign. It is a humbling experience for a mother—even one who's lived under an intense media spotlight for forty years—to watch her children excel on the world stage. Some people—including Hillary Clinton—consider the three of them to be Donald Trump's finest accomplishments. At the town-hall-style presidential debate in October last year, a man in the audience asked the candidates to mention one thing they respected about each other. Hillary said, "I respect his children. His children are incredibly able and devoted, and I think that says a lot about Donald."

I believe the credit for raising such great kids belongs to me. I was in charge of raising our children before our divorce, and I had sole custody of them after the split. I made the decisions about their education, activities, travel, child care, and allowances. When each one finished college, I said to my ex-husband, "Here is the finished product. Now it's your turn."

Donald might not have been the greatest husband to me, but he was a good father to the kids. Obviously, they adore him and are fiercely loyal to him. If he were a horrible dad, that would not be the case. If Donald wants to write a book about fatherhood, I would be happy to read it, but *Raising Trump* is my story, from my perspective, about what I did, and still do, for my family.

It wasn't easy to raise three kids as a full-time working mother, even with nannies. During my fourteen-year marriage to Donald, I designed the interiors of the Grand Hyatt Hotel and Trump Tower, was president and CEO of Trump Castle (the only woman in the top position at any casino in the world that I know of), and president and CEO of the Plaza Hotel, winning the prestigious Hotelier of the Year award in 1990. I wrote three international bestsellers and made tens of millions selling House of Ivana clothes, fragrances, and jewelry on HSN Tampa, QVC London, and TSC Canada. No matter how busy I was, I had breakfast with my children every day. I sat with them at dinner every night and helped them with their homework (I loved algebra) before going out in a Versace gown to a rubber-chicken charity event. The kids and I celebrated, traveled, and grieved together. Our bond was, and is, our most valuable possession.

By all rights, as children of divorce, surrounded by wealth and forced into fame, Don Jr., Ivanka, and Eric could have become the most damaged, druggie, poor little rich kids on the planet. Instead, the boys are devoted husbands and fathers, and are jointly running a multibillion-dollar company. Ivanka is a marvelous mother and wife; founded her own apparel, jewelry, and shoes business; authored two books (her most recent one, *Women Who Work*, I believe, was inspired by me); is now the assistant to her father, the president of the United States; and is actively working to improve the lives of women and children. I think Ivanka played a big part in Donald's victory. Voters looked at her and thought, *I like her. I trust her. She loves her father, so he can't be* that *bad.* Who knows? One day, she might be the first female—and Jewish—POTUS.

I'm often asked about the secret to mothering success, and my answer is always the same: there's no magic recipe. I told the kids, "Don't lie, cheat, or steal. Don't smoke, do drugs, or drink." I was strict and demanding but always loving and affectionate. I encouraged sports and competitiveness, and enriched their lives by exposing them to different cultures and the arts. I always held them accountable for their actions and didn't let them get away with *anything*. I showed them dignity, diligence, and determination by example, and gave them age-appropriate responsibilities and rules, which they followed without question—or there'd be hell to pay.

I raised them right and they turned out fabulous. It seems simple. And yet people are shocked that they're not train wrecks or in need of intensive therapy. Assumptions made by the public are often misguided. If *Saturday Night Live* were accurate, Don would be stiff, serious, and humorless. But he's actually very sensitive, wryly funny, and utterly smitten with his five children and his wife, Vanessa. They got Eric *completely* wrong, mistaking his niceness for naïveté. He *is* nice, yes, but he's also wise, loyal, generous, open, smart, polite, a master conversationalist, and full of energy and enthusiasm. And Ivanka. Well. People think she's all hard polish and elegance, a control freak and a little princess, but really, she's down-to-earth, empathetic, insightful, and vulnerable at times, and she cares deeply about the people she loves and the causes she supports.

I decided to share some stories about every stage of their lives, from infancy through the present, to set the record straight about who they really are. I'm also going to share some stories about my own childhood and early life so you understand exactly who I am. The mother makes the child. I learned everything I needed to know about how to be a good parent long before I became the original Mrs. Donald Trump. If you admire my children and would like to raise accomplished, ambitious winners of your own, you'll pick up some ideas from me on these pages—or from the kids themselves. Don, Ivanka, and Eric have contributed their own stories and insights, too, in boxes like this one:

———————————— IVANKA ————————————

I'm immensely proud of our mother and excited that she's written this book. She is an amazing mom, teacher, and inspiration to all of us.

Not every daughter in the world would be so excited and proud to have her mother divulge stories about her adolescence and ex-boyfriends. But Ivanka needn't worry. She was very good. If she did anything wrong, she knows I would have killed her.

———————————— ERIC ————————————

Mom was tough. She does not put up with nonsense, and I love that about her. I think her toughness is her greatest trait. She's also elegant, charming, and funny. Her personality spans a wide spectrum. There are a lot of people who may be charming but may not be as demanding. Our mom has a fun little devious laugh. She can tell a story and be so funny while conveying a toughness that commands respect.

What can I say? The kid gets me.

PART ONE

CZECH FAMILY VALUES

YOU ARE BEING WATCHED

About thirty years ago, my friend Dennis Basso, a fur designer with a then-new boutique on Madison Avenue, asked me to be the muse of his first fashion show. For the finale, I walked down the runway in a full-length sable coat. In the mid-1980s, the antifur movement was out in force, and women who wore their minks in public were sometimes splattered with red paint by PETA protesters. Some of my friends asked me if I was sure I wanted to wear fur in a fashion show. "Aren't you afraid of what the press may say?" they asked.

"No, I'm not afraid of the press," I said. "I was raised in communist Czechoslovakia. The secret police watched us constantly. We were told what to eat, where to work, how to think. I came to

America to experience freedom and opportunity. I'm going to wear what I want to wear and nobody is going to tell me otherwise."

I wore the hell out of that sable coat and had a great time doing it. Not one bad thing was written in the press about my doing the show, and even if there had been, I wouldn't have cared one tiny bit. Where I grew up, there was no free press to write articles about socialites and fashion shows. Until I was in my teens and traveled to the West as a competitive skier, I didn't know that "fashion" existed! And forget about protesting for animal—or human—rights. If you spoke out about *anything*, you'd be arrested, thrown in jail, and maybe never seen or heard from again.

So, no, I'm not afraid of anyone: not reporters, protesters, or ex-husbands. Without a doubt, my fearlessness comes from having grown up behind the Iron Curtain.

Comrade Joseph Stalin of the USSR staged a hostile takeover of the democratic Czechoslovakian government in February 1948. Anyone who fought against him was thrown in prison for life. Before I was born my home country was free and happy, and in the span of only a few months, it was dismantled by a dictator.

Exactly one year after Stalin's coup, I was born to Milos Zelnicek and Marie Zelnickova, an engineer and a telephone operator, respectively, in Zlín (the communists called it Gottwaldov), a factory town in the southeast. About 190 miles from Prague, Zlín was a town in which any influence or knowledge of the West was completely blocked out by those in charge. I arrived two months early, at only three pounds, and my parents hadn't decided on a name yet. My mother turned to the friendly woman next to her in the hospital and said, "What did you name your daughter?" She replied, "Ivana," so that's what they called me. My parents despised the

Russians, but they gave me a Russian name. Maybe they thought it would help me with the Soviets.

Before Stalin took power, my father's family was well-off. My grandmother Katrine was the president of the Bata shoe factory, the biggest employer in the region. She would go to the factory at five a.m. and be the boss all day long, while my grandfather Emmanuel stayed home to do the washing and the shopping, a gender role reversal that was unheard-of in the forties. My business acumen comes from my grandmother. My passion comes from my father, who refused to join the Communist Party despite intense pressure from the government. He kept his integrity but gave up privileges—access to better jobs, housing, and schools—that were given to loyal party members (often spies for the government). We were always watched. The police didn't arrest my father for refusing the Communist Party because he was a talented electrical engineer, and they needed his skills. I remember blueprints rolled out on the kitchen table and Dad teaching me how to read them when I was a toddler—a skill that came in handy when I worked at Trump properties and when I gut-renovated my seven-story town house on East Sixty-Fourth Street in Manhattan.

Under communism, everyone lives at the same level in one huge sprawling middle class. There aren't rich people or poor people. A doctor has the same quality of life as a farmer. (My paternal grand-parents' privilege disappeared under communism, but Katrine continued to excel at the shoe factory anyway.) You weren't allowed to go into business for yourself, open up a store, or launch a new company out of your garage. Even if you worked incredibly hard and got a big promotion, you'd have the same salary, so no one bothered. Following your bliss? Doing what you love? If that happened, it was purely accidental. No one had jobs in careers like decorating or design—or real estate. The government controlled all development and housing.

Our house was in a government compound, a two-story utilitarian box with a family upstairs and a family downstairs. These identical concrete cubes were laid out on a grid with nothing to differentiate one from the other. Each house had a tiny yard. Until I was ten, I shared a room with my parents, sleeping in a crib and then in a little bed my father built. When I was older, he built a room for me in the crawl space between the staircase and the ceiling. Nowadays, you might very generously call it a "loft." It was tiny, not roomy enough for anything but sleep, but I made it my own by putting my drawings on the walls. I didn't do much reading up there because books were hard to come by, and I didn't have time for fairy tales.

The other girls in school, the ones whose fathers were loyal party members, wore store-bought clothes. All of my dresses and tights were hand-sewn by my mother. Party members received more tickets for meat, flour, and sugar than we did and never had to resort to trading on the black market if the necessities ran out before the end of the month. We were never hungry or deprived, though, because my parents were industrious. Dad, whom I called Dedo, brought home carp and catfish he caught in the lake nearby. Mom, whom I called Babi, was a genius at foraging and storing food. My grandmother taught her to bury apples and carrots in pots full of sand to dig up all winter long. She hunted for chanterelle and porcini mushrooms in the woods, picked raspberries and blueberries to preserve in jars, and canned pears and peaches. Fresh produce in winter was nearly impossible to find. Before Christmas, you would stand in line for eight blocks to buy an orange. My father once waited for hours to get me a banana, but when he brought it home and I tried it, I didn't even like it. For my birthdays, my mother baked a cake with vanilla icing and fruit, a rare wintertime treat.

It's hard for Americans who grew up in the fifties and sixties to imagine life without TV, rock 'n' roll, and drive in movies, but we didn't have anything like that for entertainment. Elvis? Marilyn? The Beatles? We had no clue they existed. It was called the Iron Curtain for a reason. No one got out, and nothing from the West filtered in. For fun, I played with dolls that Mom made, needle-pointed tablecloths and napkins, and hung out with my best friend, a huge German shepherd named Brok with a bark like a rifle shot. I would pull his tail, put my hands over his eyes, and ride him like a horse in the yard, and he didn't care. He adored and protected me. If anyone came near me, he'd snarl and scare the hell out of them.

We had some music and books, but only what was approved by the Czech and Russian communists. Even my schoolbooks were censored. I knew America existed because the large landmass was right there on the world map, but I didn't know anything about life there. All Western ideas, especially American culture, were completely banned. We lived in a pure state of just knowing family, approved arts and literature, and sports. I didn't know what I was missing, or that there was even anything to miss.

The communists banned religion, too. My parents were raised Catholic, but if the police saw you go anywhere near a church, they would punish you by making your life harder in not-subtle ways, like stopping you on the street, coming to your house for an inspection, or withholding food tickets.

Despite our modest, careful existence, we were rich and generous with love. My parents, both drop-dead gorgeous, were madly in love with each other. They kissed all the time, but I was never embarrassed by it. I was a real daddy's girl, always hugging Dedo, crawling onto his lap, and holding his hand. Ivanka and Donald's relationship growing up reminded me of mine with my father. I thought it was totally unfair for the media to dig up old photos of them and distort their affection into something offensive. People ask me what I think of Donald's comments about how beautiful Ivanka is, and I just wave them off. His spontaneous comments have, at times, gotten him into hot water, but there was nothing inappropriate about how close they were and are. When she was younger, Ivanka sought out his attention, going to his office to see him at every chance, calling him repeatedly from a janitor's closet at school. I was the same way with Dedo. I wished I got to spend more time with him, but he always seemed to be leaving to catch the first of two buses he took to his job every day. He worked incredibly hard to give us whatever he could and to prepare me for a life where no one handed you a thing. I trusted him completely to protect me and always put me first. Both my parents treated me, their only child, like a princess. In theory, I would have liked to have had brothers and sisters, but, because I had to entertain myself, I grew up to be independent and self-sufficient.

Babi organized her life around mine. She would get up every morning at dawn to wake me, give me breakfast, help me with my homework, and braid my hair, all before I went to school. Mom's "free" hours were spent working as a phone operator at the shoe factory, shopping, cleaning, repairing, and cooking. I have no idea how hard her life would have been if she'd had more children. She picked me up at three p.m. from school and took me to afternoon sports practice before heading home to cook dinner and help me with more homework before bedtime. I was in bed at seven p.m. every night. At that hour, the same folk song came on the radio, and that was my signal to drop whatever I was doing and go to sleep.

Every summer, I would go to my maternal grandparents' farm/ vineyard in the region of Czechoslovakia called Moravia. My mother would put me on a train in the city and I had to change trains midway by myself. Mind you, I was only six years old. My grandmother Anna would pick me up on the other side. Life in the country was much easier than in Zlín. For one thing, the police weren't watching our every move, and I didn't have to get up at dawn for school or sports practice. I could play with the chickens, goats, ducks, and dogs. I remember stomping Riesling grapes to make wine. People would visit the farm to sample the wine with slices of homemade bread and bacon, and maybe buy a barrel to take home. My grandparents Anna and Vaslav took me to the summer celebrations, where twelve beautiful girls and twelve handsome boys dressed in traditional costumes and danced, and everyone baked *kolacky*, a pastry with cottage cheese in the middle and nuts or fruit on top.

I ate so well in the summers. All the food came from the farm itself. We had tomatoes, string beans, peaches, cucumbers, carrots, and lettuce. My grandmother fed the ducks corn to make their livers big. We grilled the livers and ate the duck fat on homemade bread with salt. Delicious. They raised pigs, too, and once a year, they were slaughtered and put on the spit platform by the cellar staircase to be turned into blood sausages and white sausages. Every part of the pig, snout to tail, was used. I was playing in the cellar one day when suddenly the whole pig platform collapsed. A two-hundred-pound dead animal blocked the exit, and I was stuck down there all day. I didn't mind. I had a great time eating the stores of bacon and taking bites out of the butter and bread we kept down there. When they found me, the block of butter had my tooth marks in it.

When summer ended, I returned to the city to get back to work. I had two jobs: school and sports. As a student, my grades were monitored closely because we weren't party members. If I didn't get perfect scores, I would have been kicked out and put to work in a factory. I was also an athlete from age six on, training and competing in swimming and skiing. My father pushed me into sports to make me stronger and to give me a way up and, possibly, out. In communist Czechoslovakia, there were only two ways you could excel and lift your family to a higher status. One way was playing sports and winning competitions. The other way was to be a gifted musician or ballerina. If you were good, you would be sent to other countries to compete or perform. If you were very good and won races or wowed audiences, you could earn special privileges for your family at home.

Party members, as always, had advantages in those areas, too. They got better coaches and teachers than I did. My father knew that I would be competing against well-prepared athletes, and he made me work that much harder to win. One of my earliest memories was when Dedo, a competitive swimmer himself, took me to a lake near our house, put my arms around his neck, loaded me onto his back, and started swimming. I was around four. The water was freezing—I hated cold water and still do—but I enjoyed riding on Dedo's back as he cut through the water to the middle of the lake. He loosened my arms from around his neck and dove down, emerging a few feet away from me, leaving me to tread water on my own.

He said, "Now swim back to shore."

I knew what he was up to. He'd tried to make me swim before. I said, "No!" I was a stubborn kid and he wasn't going to make me do anything I didn't want to.

"I'll give you a hundred korunas," the equivalent of five dollars.

This was new. I thought about it and said, "Okay, you've got a deal."

Swimming wasn't as horrible as I thought, and I started competing. Whenever I won, Dedo gave me an orange (in due time, our tropical fruit was imported from communist Cuba, and thus a special treat). He had to get me a lot of oranges, because I won often. When I was five, my father took me skiing for the first time, and I fell instantly in love. I started competing, and won my first race at age six. I won so often, the government took notice and watched me even more closely.

For the next five years, I was swimming or skiing whenever I wasn't in school or sleeping. I'd get up, eat, do my homework, go to the pool, swim for hours, go to school, go home, do more homework, eat dinner, and pass out by seven p.m. Every weekend, I hit the slopes and skied all day. Sports took over my mother's life, too. She had to get me to all my practices and competitions. You could compare it to an American suburban soccer mom, but Babi didn't have help at home, or reliable access to a car or money for gas, or a big-box supermarket to shop in, or frozen food, or modern appliances. She was tough as nails and never complained about her hardships once.

We lived by this hectic schedule for my entire childhood. Hard training in two sports was just what I did. I didn't question it. But when I turned thirteen, my coaches raised an issue with my father about my sports future. The goal for every athlete was to make the Olympic team. My father thought I had a shot in both sports, but the coaches said that swimming developed the upper body, and skiing was all about the legs. Bottom line: I couldn't do both. I had to choose one or the other. My parents left the decision up to me.

That weekend, we were going to our family's chalet in the mountains. "Our family's chalet" sounds more impressive than it was. It was a tiny A-frame house, and to get there you had to take a bus and then walk two miles through heavy powdered snow up the mountain. You'd walk up and ski down, no rope tow or chairlift. We went with friends and neighbors. A few men walked up first to make a trail, kids in the middle and women in the back. Everyone carried up food for the weekend in backpacks. One time, Babi brought a jar of raspberry jam to leave in the chalet, but I wanted it all for myself and snuck it back to the city in my backpack. When my father took my pack off the top of the bus, he accidentally dropped it. The hidden jar broke and covered everything with jam. He was so mad, he chased me for a mile home from the bus stop.

We were planning to go to the chalet the weekend after my father had that talk with my coaches about having to make the choice between swimming and skiing. Before we left, Dad said, "Ivana, if you want to keep swimming, stay in the city with your grandparents and go to the pool. If you want to ski, show up at the mountain tomorrow."

I didn't even have to think about it. I showed up at the mountain.

Swimming wasn't for me. It was just too boring to be underwater, surrounded by four walls. I preferred the danger of racing down an icy slope at eighty miles an hour on a pair of sticks. On the swim team, I'd go pool to pool. But on the ski team, I'd go mountain to mountain, to Italy and Austria, Switzerland and France. I'd meet Westerners and see the wonders on the other side.

I became a member of the national juniors ski team and gave the sport even more of my time and energy. As a result, my grades suffered. Bad grades put me at serious risk of being kicked out of school. So that summer, instead of going to the farm, my father put me on the assembly line at the Bata shoe factory to show me what life would be like without an education. I didn't know about Louboutins; all I knew was Bata. These were not exciting shoes, okay? The idea of working on the line making ugly and boring shoes for the rest of my life was terrifying. I begged my father to let me quit, but he made me stay until I learned my lesson. I told myself, "Over my dead body will I ever do this again." When I returned to school that fall, you better believe I got straight As.

My parents worked hard for me, and I worked just as hard for all of us. Being less than the best was simply not an option, because, in a very real way, one mistake could doom your life. We couldn't be sure who to trust outside the family. It was all too common for neighbors, teachers, and coaches to report people to the police for saying or doing the wrong thing. My childhood was defined by discipline, determination, and loyalty. I didn't know any other way to survive.

HOT PANTS, LIPSTICK, AND TANKS

When I was fourteen, the Czech juniors team went to ski camp on the Italian Matterhorn at the end of summer to start practice. It was not the Western experience I hoped for. I could have been anywhere in the world, as I saw nothing but the dorms, the trails, and the cafeteria. Every move we made was watched by the communist coaches and trainers. The skiers weren't allowed to leave their rooms without a police escort. We woke up at dawn to go straight to the mountain to train for three hours. My events were slalom (skiing between tightly arranged poles), giant slalom (skiing between more spread-out poles), and, my specialty, downhill (skiing as fast as possible straight down the mountain). I'd race through the course, take the lift back to the top, and do it again, over and over. When the sun was high and the snow got heavy, we would go to the bottom of the mountain for sprints and weight training with the coaches. After lunch, we were back on the mountain, racing until the sun went down and the slopes turned to sheer ice that would crunch and crack under your skis.

My life was ski, ski, eat, run, train, ski, eat, sleep. I was a prisoner of the system and felt rightly trapped in it, but at least I was alive and free in the exhilaration, speed, and danger while racing. I pushed myself hard to be fast and win. If I didn't, I might have been kicked off the team. If you added even a few seconds to your time, you might lose your spot. If you had a serious fall and broke a bone, you were gone. Good-bye to travel, good-bye to special privileges for your family, hello to the assembly line for life.

The team went to Vienna, Austria, which was only two hours from my hometown, but it might as well have been a different planet. At a market, I saw a strawberry in February for the first time. I couldn't believe my eyes. People could have fresh fruit in winter? This was available to everyone? The entire market amazed me. Fruits and vegetables of every kind and color, things I'd never seen before, butchers with dozens of cuts of meat in cases, and people from all walks of life just going into the shop, buying whatever they wanted, and taking it home in a brown wax-paper bundle.

I was in awe of all the beautiful things in Vienna: the stylish clothes on the women walking down the street; stores selling books, furniture, art, musical instruments, hats, beautiful shoes (no Bata there), candy, chocolate, pretzels, beer—so much beer; and restaurants full of happy, laughing people holding menus with endless options. I walked around the city with my jaw perpetually open. The variety astonished me. I'd had no idea that such abundance existed. For me, luxury was salt. Veal once a month was extravagant.

But here, there were cakes and champagne, enormous shiny cars and fur coats. This was the better life on the other side. On that day I swore that I'd live it.

When I was seventeen, I moved to Prague to study at Charles University, the oldest university in central Europe, founded in 1348 (three hundred years before Harvard). If not for my grades and skiing, I never would have been permitted to go there to study German and English, languages that would help lay the world at my feet. I was a few hours from home, but I felt safe in the city on my own.

At that time, Czechoslovakia was starting to wake up from a long Soviet winter in what became known as the Prague Spring. A political reformer named Alexander Dubček was elected as first secretary of the Communist Party in Czechoslovakia, and he cut back on restrictions in the arts and media, public speech, and travel. As a result, our capital was booming with new culture and ideas, challenging the oppression of the past two decades. Cafés and dance halls opened. People were reading illicit materials and writing their own. New music filtered into our world, and I was right in the middle of the cultural revolution.

I was still closely watched, of course. As well as being on the university ski team, I started modeling and acting. I was getting to be a little famous at school—but the government had ways of making sure you knew who was really in control. Every time I came back from a sporting event in the West, I had to report to the police station for a two-hour "interview" (really, an interrogation) by the communists. I'd sit down on a metal chair in a room with white walls, and two men would ask me the same questions each time: "What did people wear?" "What did they eat?" "What did they say?"

I'd let them pick my brain and answered the questions, keeping my replies factual and short, and my true feelings under lock and key. If I acted too excited about seeing a strawberry in winter in Vienna, they might worry about a defection and not let me travel again. Pretending to be nonchalant was good training for dealing with the media later on in my life, but it also conditioned me to block and hide my emotions. To this day, it's very hard for me to let any vulnerability show.

After an hour of questioning, they'd let me go. "Okay, Ivana. See you next month," they'd say, and I'd slowly walk out of there. I wanted to run.

Over time, I got to know the interviewers pretty well because I was traveling so much for skiing and came to see them less as enemies and more as regular people just doing their jobs. I started to bring them back presents from my travels—chewing gum, cigarettes, lipsticks, and panty hose for their girlfriends—and my interviews got a lot shorter. My father's trick of offering me the equivalent of five dollars to swim to shore paid off for me in that white room. A little bribery worked wonders.

Sex was forbidden for skiers. If the coaches found out that you were doing it, you were kicked off. Same thing with alcohol. One beer was enough to warrant permanent ejection. At the time, I had a boyfriend named George and we kept our romance a secret, but not our friendship. We trained together, running up and down steps in town and through the woods for a rendezvous. I had some money for the first time in my life, thanks to our Austrian sponsors,

Fischer and Atomic Skis. I bought a navy Fiat 500, and George got a BMW. We had to maintain our grades at school, but we were given a special exam schedule. I was on the mountains from August to April, so I took all my exams in May, June, and July. I would cram a year's worth of information into my head in a week, ace the test, and then forget it all the next day. At school, we had a special dining room and were given tickets daily for lunches and dinners, but because I was away so much and had so many extra tickets, I would invite all my friends—artists, musicians, and architects, the devils of Prague—to the dining room so they could eat veal, chicken, and fresh veggies that they normally couldn't get.

Athletes were treated like national heroes and were given a lot of leeway. As long as I was on the ski team, I could park my Fiat anywhere in town. Once, I parked too close to the tram tracks, and a bunch of men got off the tram, lifted up the car, and moved it one meter to the left. There was a tunnel by my school that, if I went through it, would get me from my house to the school's front door in five minutes. But the tunnel was closed going in that direction, so you had to go around, adding twenty minutes to the trip. I would wait until a tram came by and then drive alongside it in the illegal direction. The police on the other side couldn't see me. I did this for years before a cop finally pulled me over.

I played the little country girl in my hot pants and leather boots (fashion choices that were possible thanks to Dubček's reforms) and started to cry. I said, "Officer! I'm lost!"

He said, "You've been doing it for years, and now you're going to pay!"

So much for my act.

He gave me a ticket, and kept giving them to me whenever

he caught me. The next time I went to the police station for my post-travel interview, I handed over a carton of cigarettes and panty hose, and a big stack of parking and traffic tickets. I said, "I was so busy skiing and doing my homework, I forgot to pay these." The fines could amount to the equivalent of a hundred dollars.

The head cop would put my gifts in his desk drawer and say, "Okay, Ivana. You still have to pay your fines. Give me two hundred korunas," or about ten bucks.

I was a good student and decided to continue on with school to get my master's in physical education. I stayed on the ski team as well. In 1968, the Prague Spring rolled into summer. I was supposed to go to Cervinia for ski camp soon, but I hated to leave my friends in the city when we were having so much fun. But the Russians didn't like the Czech people to think and learn, or to forget who was in charge. In August, five thousand Soviet tanks rolled into Wenceslas Square, the cultural and historical heart of Prague. Two hundred thousand Soviet and other Warsaw Pact countries' soldiers invaded the city, intent on reasserting control, crushing the new sense of freedom, and ousting Dubček. At Radio Prague, the workers refused to let the communists take over the station, and twenty people were executed on the spot. Government leaders who resisted were rounded up and sent to Moscow—to be tortured and killed, no doubt. Over one hundred protesters, students similar to me and my friends, were murdered where they stood on the street. It was one of the biggest foreign invasions since World War II.

Prague was mayhem, a living nightmare. I saw the tanks arrive and ran to hide in the university dorms. The next day, when the team took a train to Italy, I was on it. We stayed in Cervinia for two weeks and managed to get our hands on newspapers to learn what was happening in Prague. It scared the daylights out of me. I thought long and hard about defecting to Italy then and there, but that would mean I'd never see my family again, and that they'd be in trouble with the government, especially now. I couldn't be responsible for their suffering, so I returned to Prague and was heartbroken by the change. The cafés and clubs were closed. The music had stopped. People were afraid to be out in public. No wonder: the streets were crawling with hard-line communist police and soldiers.

George and I talked about how we were going to escape. His opportunity came sooner than either of us expected. His father was an architect and was designing the Czech embassy in London. When his family came back to Prague from England, they told George they were going to defect and wanted to bring him with them. Who could blame him for choosing to go?

Before he left, George came up with a plan for me. We were friends with an Austrian skier named Alfred (Fred) Winklmayr. If Fred and I got married, I'd have an Austrian passport and would be able to leave communist Czechoslovakia legally and still be able to see my family. The marriage wouldn't be real, of course, and Fred had no illusion that it meant anything. It was only for me to get the necessary papers. Why did he go along with it? He was a friend and he wanted to make a noble gesture to help someone flee an oppressive regime. He came to Prague and we married in a government building in 1971 when I was twenty-two. (We stayed married for two years to fool the government, and divorced in 1973 as soon as it was safe.) After the ceremony, Fred returned to Vienna and I waited for a month for my Austrian passport to arrive. George was at the wedding, but he left shortly after to meet his parents in

London and went on to Canada from there. Our farewell wasn't a time to cry or be sad. He was getting out! Instead, we celebrated his freedom.

When he left Prague, I lost my best friend and felt very alone, but I was relieved and happy for him that he got out. Even though I had a new passport, I couldn't leave yet. I was halfway toward getting my master's, and I couldn't walk away now. I was the only child in my family, and my parents counted on me. I needed that degree to elevate myself, and then I'd be in a position to help them. I loved George and missed him, but I didn't dwell on my loneliness. I stayed focused on my goals for myself and my duty to my parents, and looked ahead to the future, when I would hopefully see him again. Whenever the loneliness crept into my thoughts, I pushed it away by keeping busy. I worked harder at school and continued to ski. When a friend's pet poodle had puppies, he gave me a little black one. I named him Chappy, and he became my constant companion.

Soon enough, loneliness stopped being an issue at all. I had my dog, and several months after that, I fell in love.

I met Jiří Štaidl, a musician and a poet, through mutual friends. His brother Ladislav (Lada) wrote the tunes, Jiří wrote the lyrics, and legendary Czech singer Karel Gott recorded them, earning the brothers respect, fame, and money. Jiří wasn't an athletic type at all. He was kind of chubby and had no discipline for sports or exercise. But he was talented and sweet, and he made me laugh. We were deeply in love, and I became his muse. We'd often go to Lada's villa in Jevany on the weekends. While I studied, he'd be at the typewriter. From the other room, I'd hear *tap, tap, tap*, and I knew he'd found the words for a new song, probably about me. We were both swept up in our romance, and being with Jiří made me realize that what George and I had was a very close friendship but not true love. Jiří was the real deal. Even though I had my escape papers, I couldn't leave him behind.

In 1973, I had to go to Vienna to complete some paperwork related to a skiing competition and made the short trip by myself. When I got back to Prague, I went to my police interview as usual—"Yes, Austria is pretty. Yes, women wear nice clothes and perfume. Here's a bottle for your wife!" Then I went to the bistro where Jiří was picking me up so we could drive to Jevany together, where we could have peace and quiet. He had ten songs to write and I had exams to study for. But he never arrived. I soon learned that, while driving around on some errands, he'd gotten in a car accident and died.

The details of the accident were murky and I couldn't get an explanation of what had happened from his family. It's possible he'd had a drink or two before he got behind the wheel, but I don't know for sure. He was only thirty and so talented. It was a horrible, tragic end to a bright young life.

I was devastated, just destroyed. The man who had made life a song, who had made living under communism bearable, was now gone. I'd lost my love in a moment, and because of the mysterious circumstances of his death, I didn't have closure. One minute, he was there at my side, and the next he was gone, and I wasn't supposed to ask or talk about it. I was very young, in my early twenties, and a loss that big was more than I could handle. I suffered panic attacks and thought I was dying of a broken heart.

I returned to the pillars of strength that had gotten me through every hardship thus far (and the ones yet to come): my parents. I went home and cried on their shoulders and let them comfort me. My father reminded me of my goals: to finish my education and to leave legally so that I could have a better life in a free country. That had been their plan for me since I was born. After Jiří's death, the only thing tethering me to Czechoslovakia was my parents, and they wanted nothing more than for me to start from scratch somewhere else. Once I got settled, they could visit me. Having this clear plan gave me something to think about other than my pain. The deep loss was always there, but at least I could escape it by fantasizing about a new life.

In the fog of heartache, I waded through the last of my classes. I put on a brave face because I had no other choice, and because that was what I'd been conditioned to do for so long. I got through Jiří's funeral but I couldn't bear seeing the musicians, artists, and painters who were our friends in the weeks afterward. I didn't want to go to the same places or eat at the same restaurants. Some of Jiří's friends actually tried to make a move on me, and it made me hate them all, hate Prague, and feel desperate to leave. Even after all these years, recalling that time is deeply upsetting. I've sent flowers to his grave on the anniversary of his death every single year.

The day Jiří's life ended, so did my life in Prague. As soon as I got my degree, I grabbed my passport, put my suitcase in the Fiat, drove to the airport with Chappy, and we were off: first, a short stop in Vienna, and then, eventually, to my new home.

WELCOME TO AMERICA

Dreaming of freedom got me though Jiří's death more than anything else. The question was, where in the world should I go? I could move to Europe. I knew people through the skiing community, but that wouldn't be a complete break. The gravitational pull of my parents so close by would have tempted me to come home to them, and then I might have wound up staying forever. Czechoslovakia is a beautiful country, with great food and wonderful people, but after the invasion of Prague and my lover's death, I needed to put an ocean between us.

My father's sister and her husband lived in Toronto, Canada, in a big house in the prestigious part of town called Forest Hill. They offered to let Chappy and me stay with them for a while. Touching down in Toronto, I felt only relief that my old life was over and excitement about starting a new one. The farther I got from Prague and memories of Jiří, the easier it was to breathe.

Driving through the city from the airport, I noticed that in some neighborhoods the houses were smaller and closer together. In others, they were larger and farther apart. I'd never seen suburban class divides before. Unlike Czechoslovakians, the people there weren't locked into one class from birth to death. You could conceivably change your life in the West if you had a big idea, a big job, or big dreams. It was all about BIG.

The scale of everything, from the houses to the streets, seemed supersized. In Europe, the streets are narrow and many of them can only fit one car at a time. But in Canada, there were four-lane highways, giant trucks, brawny people, skyscrapers, shopping malls that were the size of a whole city block, and ten-story parking garages. You could walk from the garage into the mall, spend a whole day there, go back to your car, and never once step outside.

Everything was new to me. The excitement of it all kept me from feeling homesick, and it helped that, because I'd left legally, my parents would be permitted to visit me. (After Czech tennis superstars Martina Navratilova and Ivan Lendl defected, they didn't see their families for years.) The first goal for my new life was to get a job and make enough money to send my parents plane tickets. They had to see all this.

My uncle was an architect, and my aunt ran Costa Line, a Toronto-based cruise line that gave tours in Europe and the Caribbean. They took me on a Caribbean cruise shortly after I arrived. On the first night, there was a costume party on the boat. I was twenty-four, really cute, and dressed as a Playboy Bunny—and I won first prize! I met a sailor on the cruise who was very attentive and I was pretty sure he was flirting with me, although my English wasn't so great then. I needed friends, so I agreed to go on a date with him. Despite everything I'd learned about being on guard in Czechoslovakia, this sailor had me fooled. I thought he was just a nice boy who would treat me with respect. Instead, he invited me to his cabin and tried to rape me. As soon as the door was closed, he rushed at me, put his hands all over me, and tried to rip off my clothes.

I'd never been assaulted before, and it was much scarier than any communist interrogation. I was literally trapped. This sailor meant to do me physical harm. My life was under threat, and this experience was a new kind of fear. I started screaming, "Let me go!" and used every muscle I had to fight my way out of the cabin. I ran into the corridor, still screaming, and found my way to the safety of my own cabin.

I learned that night that freedom had many textures, and some of them were rough. I'd been fighting against a big nebulous enemy for so long—communism—and that night, I realized there were individual, more concrete threats that could also do terrible harm. Just because I was in a free country didn't mean that I could ignore certain aspects and terrors of life. I'd never been physically threatened before. I learned a hard but important lesson: you have to be on your guard and protect yourself, and politeness and naïveté could put you in scary situations. As strong as I was mentally and physically, I was still vulnerable. From that day on, I honed my instincts regarding people and trained myself to listen to my inner warning system.

For the year and a half I lived with my relatives, I studied

English and started modeling. I'd done some modeling in Prague already and hadn't thought of pursuing it in Canada—but opportunity knocked when a nicely dressed woman came up to me in a coffee shop in Toronto and introduced herself as an agent with William Morris. "I'd like to represent you," she said. I thought, *Why not?* I checked her out to make sure she was legitimate, and then I started taking jobs in Toronto. She suggested that I could get even more work in Montreal. So, at twenty-six, I moved again.

George (remember him?) lived in Montreal with his parents, so Chappy and I went to live with his family. I hadn't seen him in a few years, but it was like we'd never parted. We rekindled our college romance, half-heartedly at best. Our friendship was as strong as it had been when we were teenagers, though, and it was the most natural thing to be together again. His parents made me feel loved and welcome, too.

On winter weekends, George and I went to Jay Peak resort in Vermont, a two-hour drive from Montreal. American skiing was very different than competing in Europe. The snow is dry here, and much lighter than in France or Italy. I was used to pushing around heavy, wet powder. The powder in Vermont was up to my waist, but it was so light, I could ski circles around the Americans. In no time, I became a ski instructor at Jay Peak and taught kids how to race.

Canada, in case you don't know, is freaking *cold*! The temperature could drop to sixty-four below with the windchill factor. I drove a Fiat X1/9 sports car, praying all winter I wouldn't get stuck in a snowbank or skid into a ditch. On the mountain, I shivered constantly in my skimpy ski suit, with a sleek jacket and tights underneath the pants. I could have worn warmer clothes, but I don't participate in a sport if I can't look elegant. To warm up, I just skied harder.

George and I rented a chalet with three other couples for weekends and vacations. I always brought along Chappy. That caused some tension in the house because the other couples refused to let him sleep inside. I had to leave him in the car buried under piles of blankets overnight. In the morning, the windows on the inside were frozen with ice from his breathing. We cooked dinners for eight in the chalet, and I showed off my mother's recipes for goulash and chicken paprika. In the summers, we'd go get fresh lobsters, but I refused to cook the lobsters myself. When you throw them into the boiling water, they squeak. I couldn't stand the sound, but succulent lobster with melted lemon butter was fabulous.

The modeling agent was right: I had a lot of opportunities in Montreal, starting with a full-time job at the Vali showroom. The designer, Audrey, was also from Czechoslovakia, and we bonded instantly. My job was to model her clothes in the showroom for department store buyers. They'd look at me in the dresses and place big orders. My agent also connected me to Yolande Cardinal, the woman in charge of booking all the models for fashion shows in Montreal. (Yolande and I remained friends. I once helped her find a doctor in America when one of her children had a health crisis. She still writes to me and keeps me up-to-date on her family.) A furrier in Montreal hired me to be the face of his company, and I modeled his coats and jackets in advertising campaigns, as well as in magazine and newspaper articles about the company.

When I wasn't skiing, modeling, or helping George at the little sports shop he opened to sell and repair skis in the winter and bikes in the summer, I took some English classes at McGill University. We were doing very well and had enough money to move out of George's parents' house and into a rental apartment in Château Maisonneuve, a cute place in a nice neighborhood. I didn't care about being wealthy. If I had a job, could pay my bills, and wasn't poor, I was happy. I didn't have career goals or a five year plan. Whatever my job was, I would do my best. If I were a salesperson at the Eaton mall, I'd put my Czech into it, and in six months, I'd be a manager. In two years, I'd own the place. George and I had a good life. I wasn't thinking about getting married and becoming a Canadian hockey mom or learning to sugar my own maple syrup. I was just settling into my freedom.

A few years after I immigrated, my agent booked me as part of a group of eight models for a show of Canadian designers to promote the '76 Montreal Summer Olympics. It sounded like a good gig, so I said yes. Then they told me that we had to go to New York for a weekend and do the show there, and I said no. My father had just arrived from Czechoslovakia to be with me. I wasn't going to leave him, even for a few days. But the booker said that the show was choreographed, which I knew, and that they couldn't find anyone to replace me. If I didn't go, I'd ruin it for everyone else.

What could I do? I said good-bye to my father and George, packed my bags, and got on a plane bound for New York City. I had no idea what—and who—I'd find there.

PART TWO

BECOMING A TRUMP

4

HOW I MET THEIR FATHER

It was love at first sight, the powerful, instant thrill of realizing we were born to be together and that our passion would never fade.

I'm talking about New York City, of course. As soon as I saw it for the first time, I knew I'd found a place with an energy that matched my own. It was just spectacular. I thought the skyscrapers in Montreal were impressive, but the ones in New York put them to shame. I was a typical tourist, staring up at the tall buildings, the yellow cabs, the incredible diversity of the people on the street. I wanted to explore every block, the art museums, discos, concert halls, restaurants, and stores. New York was pure adrenaline: big, bold, and loud. I wasn't sure about living there (yet), but I was thrilled to visit.

Our travel for the fashion show was all taken care of: flights, hotels, everything. We were booked at the Americana on Seventh Avenue, a hotel with fifty-three floors and a storied history. The Beatles once performed at the on-site nightclub, and scenes from *The Godfather* were filmed there (by that point, I'd learned about rock music and gangster movies, so I was impressed). The other girls and I spent the day walking around the city in the July heat, which was exciting and exhausting. When we got back to the hotel that first evening, I was ready for air-conditioning, room service, and bed. We had early rehearsals the next day, but my friends *really* wanted to go out and see the swinging seventies singles scene. "Come *on*, Ivana! We're in New York City!" they said. I let them convince me, but I wasn't fully into it.

We went to Maxwell's Plum, which was the hottest restaurant in the city at the time, famous for its chili, burgers, and celebrity clientele. The girls were hoping to see Warren Beatty or Barbra Streisand, and maybe meet some sexy American men, but I didn't care. I was living with George, happy with my life, and not on the hunt for true love or a fling. Really, I wasn't interested in anything but dinner.

Isn't it true of life that when you're not looking for something, it walks right up and taps you on the shoulder?

While we stood at the maître d' stand, the girls scanned the crowd for cute guys, and I took in the chaotic, decadent décor—red velvet; crystal; Tiffany chandeliers; a stained-glass ceiling in crazy, colorful patterns; stuffed tigers and animals hanging from the walls; packed tables; a crush of people at the bar, everyone done up to the nines in slinky, sexy dresses and glam makeup.

I was wearing a red minidress with three-quarter sleeves and high heels. My blond hair was long and straight, swinging all the way down to my waist. All of the girls in the group looked great. The maître d' practically rubbed his hands together with glee when he saw us. I could see the wheels turning. *Eight beautiful models, together?* I knew he'd try to keep us there all night, as visible as possible. Sure enough, when we asked for a table, he brought us to the middle of the bar and said it'd be a bit of a wait. I was tired and hungry, and my mood was going from bad to worse.

Then I felt a hand on my arm.

Now this? I thought. I did *not* like to be touched by strangers in bars. I spun around, ready to give the hand's owner the commie death stare, and found a tall, smiling, blue-eyed, handsome blond man.

He said, "I am so sorry to bother you. My name is Donald Trump, and I noticed that you and your friends are waiting for a table. I know the manager and I can get you one fast."

"That would be great," I replied. "Thank you." He went off to take care of it. I turned back to my friends and said, "I have good news and bad news. The good news is that we are going to have a table soon because of that man over there."

One of the girls asked, "What's the bad news?"

"He's going to sit with us."

Three minutes later, we had the best table in the place, and this Donald Trump sat down next to me. The waiter came and took our orders. None of the models were having wine or cocktails because we had an early call the next day. I was surprised that Donald didn't drink, either. He asked for an iced tea. The meal was fine—I had chicken paillard, and he had a burger—and we made polite small talk, no funny stuff at all. He sensed correctly that flirting would not work with me and acted like a gentleman. I can spot a bullshit artist from three blocks away. My instincts told me that Donald was smart and funny—an all-American good guy.

As we were finishing our dinner, he disappeared from the table without a word, which was strange. We asked the waiter for the bill, and he said, "It's been taken care of." I thought, *What's going on?* A man pays a $400 bill for nine people—very discreetly, which I liked—and then doesn't expect something in return? Donald didn't even say good-bye!

We talked about whether we should wait for him to return so we could thank him, or just leave. After ten minutes, we decided to go. We exited the restaurant, and at the curb, we saw Donald behind the wheel of a big, black Cadillac limousine. He'd run to his building, where he and his driver kept a limo, and returned to the restaurant to chauffeur us back to our hotel in style. Seeing him sitting in the driver's seat with a silly grin on his face struck me as funny, and I started laughing. He saw my reaction and started laughing, too. We all piled into the limo, and he drove us to our hotel. I got out of the car and, before heading up to my room, leaned into the car window to give him a polite kiss on the cheek. I thought that was the end of that.

The next day, one hundred red roses arrived at the hotel with a note: "To Ivana, with affection. Donald." The arrangement and the gesture were lovely, but I wasn't a blushing virgin who'd never been sent flowers before. I was twenty-seven and had been hit on by countless men since the age of fourteen. I knew every seduction trick in the book.

I thought, *He's going to call me in five . . . four . . . three . . . two . . .*

Ring. I picked up the phone and said coyly, "Hello?"

It was Donald, inviting me to lunch. I had the fashion show that afternoon, so he upgraded to dinner.

He took me to a private club with the not-too-original name Le Club on East Fifty-Eighth Street, a favorite hot spot of Mike Nichols, Roy Cohn, Jacqueline Kennedy, and Al Pacino, to name a few, and introduced me to the manager, a giant man named Patrick Shields. I was wearing sexy harem pants and a red blouse with a floral pattern; Donald wore a three-piece suit with a tie and pocket square. He looked like a smart businessman, which, I was coming to realize, was his look.

It was a slow Monday night, and it seemed like we had Le Club to ourselves. We sat on the upstairs balcony, had a nice dinner, watched the Olympics on TV, and talked about the athletes. It was the summer of Nadia Comaneci of Romania and her perfect ten, Princess Anne's riding for England (she was the only athlete not forced to take a test to prove her gender), and Bruce Jenner's dominance in the decathlon. Donald told me about working at a construction site with his father, Fred Trump, and how he commuted from Manhattan to Queens every morning. At the time, he lived in Phoenix House on East Sixty-Fifth Street and Third Avenue.

I listened to Donald and held up my end of the conversation, but I didn't feel a special affinity for him. He was just a nice guy, a gentleman, someone to spend an evening with for easy conversation and a pleasant meal. I thought, *If I never see him again, it's fine.* But Donald had other ideas. "Have dinner with me tomorrow," he said when he dropped me off at the hotel. I couldn't. Our flight back to Montreal left in the late afternoon. "Then have lunch with me."

The guy didn't quit! I agreed to meet him at another swanky restaurant, the '21' Club on East Fifty-Second Street, known for its steak and the chorus line of cast-iron lawn jockeys on the balcony above the front door, for a quick lunch. It was our third meal in as many days. When we said good-bye, he kissed the back of my hand.

It was very chaste. Donald was the first American I'd dated, and he struck me as shy and respectful compared to European men, who would move in and go for it before the appetizers had arrived. Donald was aggressive about only one thing: getting my phone number. Honestly, I didn't see the point. I was going home to my sort-of boyfriend in another city, another country. This Donald (he was "this Donald" before I dubbed him "the Donald") had a city full of beautiful women to choose from in New York. I expected him to think about me for another day or two and then lose my number. But in the meantime, I gave it to him just to make him stop asking.

He called the day after I got home, and every other day for the next three months. It created some tension for me at home because I hadn't told George about Donald, or Donald about George, so I breathed a sigh of relief whenever Donald called when George was out. I rushed him off the phone a few times when I heard the apartment door open and George shout out, "I'm home!" I found myself looking forward to hearing from Donald, and I saved up things to tell him about my day.

In October, I was walking the runway in a fur coat at a fashion show in Montreal, and I happened to notice a tall blond man in the audience. Our eyes met, and he smiled at me. Donald was at the show? He'd somehow found out about it and come to Montreal to surprise me. It made me slightly uncomfortable that he had information about me that I didn't give him—a hangover from a communist childhood, perhaps—but I was also flattered. I had to stay after the show to do some photographs for the furrier. When it was over and I went outside, I half expected to find Donald waiting for me at the curb behind the wheel of a limo. But he was gone, like a ghost.

The strangeness of his appearance and subsequent disappearance started to have an effect on me. I thought about him more and more. He wasn't in my heart yet, but I was starting to like him and felt intrigued by him. We had the same kind of drive and energy. Not a lot of people are like us, and we recognized those qualities in each other.

Around Christmas, he called to tell me that he'd like to take me on a vacation. "Beach or mountains?" he asked.

I said, "I always had white Christmases in my country. I'll take mountains." Donald suggested Aspen, and I agreed. I knew some people there, including my friend Tony, an Austrian skier from the old days who owned a ski school and a boutique in the center of town.

One day while we were planning our vacation, George answered the phone when I was out and "met" Donald unexpectedly. Later, when George confronted me, I rightly described Donald as a friend. We hadn't even kissed or talked face-to-face since the summer. George and I had known each other for so long that he sensed there was something serious going on with Donald before I did. When I told him about our holiday rendezvous in Aspen, George took it well. Our friendship was too old and deep for jealousy. He gave me his blessing.

Donald arranged all the details: the first-class plane tickets and the reservation at a Chris Hemmeter–built luxury chalet very close to the ski lift with a breathtaking mountain view, a fireplace, mirrors on the ceiling, and a chinchilla throw on the bed. It was a *very* sexy chalet. I knew Donald had picked it for my benefit. I'm a realist, but I have a strong romantic streak and can see the moon and the stars. Donald wouldn't see the moon if it were sitting on his chest.

The suite had two bedrooms, by the way.

I hadn't decided about where I would sleep yet, but after seeing the place, I made up my mind pretty quickly. I'd made a clear, conscious choice to be there with him. I could have said no to his dinner invitations, his constant phone calls, this trip—to everything—but I kept saying yes to all of it.

The first morning of our vacation, Donald asked me, "Do you know how to ski?"

I almost choked on my coffee. Somehow, in all our meals together and phone conversations, we'd never gotten around to talking about skiing. How was that even possible? It seemed like a major gap in my life story that he wasn't aware of.

I shrugged and said, "I'm okay."

He had little experience and took some lessons the first day. We hit the slopes together on the second day, and he saw just how "okay" I was. While watching me fly down the mountain, he decided that he was going to become as good a skier as I was. Even he would admit his skiing never reached expert level, but he improved as the sport became important to him—and eventually to the kids as well. Christmas in Aspen would become our favorite family tradition.

We had a blissful week of skiing, enjoying our chalet and each other. It was the most romantic time of my life thus far. He must have felt the same way, because on New Year's Eve, he said to me over dinner, "If you don't marry me, you'll ruin your life."

I might've laughed, and then I saw the expression on his face. I realized, *Oh my God. He's serious.* We had chemistry, similar drives, but the truth was, we barely knew each other. We'd met only a few months ago, and for most of that time, we'd been apart.

I was turning twenty-eight the following month, and I knew I'd have to get married soon if I wanted to have children (I definitely did). Did I want to share my life with the Donald? I was falling for him, but was that enough? During my years as a model in Montreal, I'd had my pick of wealthy men, and they'd all left me cold with their entitlement and superior attitude. But Donald liked simple food and simple pleasures. Back then, he was working for his father and his income was modest compared to what he would be making several years later. He wasn't offering me fabulous riches, only love, friendship, and a two-carat diamond ring. As an athlete, I'd learned to trust my instincts and to go with them without hesitation. My gut told me that Donald was trustworthy and that he'd be a good provider.

"My life is saved," I said. "I'll marry you."

"How about February?"

Next month? "You're crazy," I said, laughing. I needed more than a few weeks to plan a wedding! I hadn't met his family or told my parents about him. We had to figure out where we were going to live, for starters. There were too many things to do first. He agreed to wait until April.

For anyone counting, my move to New York would be my

fourth relocation and third country of residence in seven years. From Aspen, I went back to Montreal; packed my bags; said a tearful good-bye to George, who remains, to this day, my oldest and dearest friend; and hopped another plane to New York to start yet another brand-new life.

MEET THE TRUMPS

I didn't have a job, friends, or family in New York, and for the first few months, I wasn't so sure I'd made the right decision. Rebuilding from scratch wasn't ever easy, and I found New Yorkers not as warm and welcoming as Canadians. The city had its own mysterious customs and codes to figure out, but I was a fast learner and adapter. I knew I'd get the hang of it soon enough.

I started going out with Donald to his swanky hangouts, like Le Club, '21,' Elaine's, and Regine's, restaurants and discos where rich and famous trendsetters dressed fabulously, gossiped about each other, drank, and did drugs. I had a glass of champagne or wine but turned my nose up at (and away from) cocaine, which was as abundant in New York as snow in Aspen. Donald never touched a drop of alcohol or any drugs.

A real test of my first months of being in Donald's world was when I met his family at a big brunch at Tavern on the Green, a beloved New York institution at Central Park West and Sixty-Seventh Street. Donald gave me a rundown of who'd be there and the gentle warning that they'd all be checking me out, the new fiancée. I probably wasn't what they expected for him. For all I knew, his parents had hoped he'd propose to an American from a wealthy family or a graduate of his college, the University of Pennsylvania ("What is this thing you call 'Ivy League'?" I asked Donald once). Regardless, I would do my best to win them over. Having been an only child, I was curious what it would be like to be part of a big, close family.

The entire Trump clan arrived exactly on time. I learned early on that they were punctual to an extreme. For them, "on time" meant five minutes early. When Donald arrived in a boardroom, or took his seat on an airplane and the door closed, that was that. If you weren't on the inside, the meeting or the flight would start without you. Donald once left Don Jr. standing on the tarmac for being five minutes late to the airport.

I think Donald was more nervous than I was when he introduced me to his family. I shook hands and smiled at his father, Fred, and mother, Mary; his sisters, Maryanne, who became a United States district court judge, and Elizabeth, an assistant to a banker; his brothers, Fred Jr., a pilot, and Robert, also in the family business; and all of their spouses and children.

We sat at a long table. I was the only one to glance at the menu. The waiter came over to take our orders, and Fred started off, saying, "I'll have the steak."

Mary said, "The steak, please."

The sisters and brothers and kids said, "Steak, steak, steak . . ."

Was there an echo in the room?

Donald said, "I'll have"—wait for it—"*the steak.*"

I love a big juicy steak as much as anyone—but at eleven a.m.? No, thank you. When the waiter got to me, I said, "Could I please have the fillet of sole?"

Next to me, Donald cringed.

Fred said, "No, she'll have the steak."

I said, with a smile, "No, I'll have the fillet of sole."

The poor waiter didn't know what to do. He looked back and forth, and finally just left. Meanwhile, the table had gone dead silent. Nobody said a word for at least three minutes. What was going on? In the Trump family, was it a law that you had to eat meat at brunch?

I just kept smiling.

Eventually, someone started talking and the mood lightened. When the food arrived, Fred pointedly asked me, "How's the fish, Ivana?"

"Delicious, thank you," I said.

When we got home later, Donald asked, "Why didn't you just have a friggin' steak? Who cares?"

"No," I responded, "if I just go along with everything he says from the beginning, your father is going to control our lives," I said.

I understood the concept of a strong father being the leader of the family, but a man who insisted you eat food you didn't want? That was too much. I didn't fight my way out of Czechoslovakia and move to the greatest city in the world to be told what I could and couldn't order at brunch. As it turned out, one mini-rebellion was enough. From that day on, Fred would give me little tests to see how far I'd go to challenge him. He'd point at the wall and say, "The wall is green. What do you think, Ivana?"

I'd reply, "That wall is *not* green, Fred. It's beige." Then he'd beam at me. Fred seemed to get a kick out of my contradicting him. Not many people challenged him.

What he did *not* like about me, however, was how I dressed. Compared to me in my tight bustier sheaths that showed off my décolleté and a lot of leg, Elizabeth and Maryanne looked almost like nuns in long-sleeved dresses with high collars and low hems. I, however, would go to a black-tie dinner at the Waldorf Astoria in a cleavage-baring, sleeveless Versace gown, and Fred's eyes would pop out of his head.

"Donald, can you give Ivana some money so that she can buy a dress with enough fabric to cover her arms?" Fred asked.

Donald would just laugh it off but suggested I dress a bit more modestly when I saw Fred. I said, "Okay, I'm going to make your father happy."

At the next event that we attended together, I wore a halter dress that revealed my arms but had a high neck and went all the way down to the floor.

Fred said, "Ivana! You look so good tonight."

"Thank you, Fred." And then I turned around so he could see that the dress was backless and dipped all the way down to my G-string.

I heard him say, "Oh my God," as I walked away laughing.

Mary, Donald's mother, was a doll. She had a charming Scottish accent and the biggest heart in the world. She raised her five children by herself in their Queens home without the help of nannies, housekeepers, or cooks. I have no idea how she did it. All of the Trumps (with rare exceptions) were driven, ambitious people who believed in the American dream: that if you worked hard, you would succeed. None of them worked harder than Mary. Like my mother, Mary was sustained and supported by the obvious love and affection of her husband and the devotion of her children.

Mary was kind and patient; Fred was demanding and opinionated. The combination of tender and tough was an excellent parenting formula. Later on, when I became a mother, my style was to be like Fred and Mary rolled into one, both adoring and exacting.

Despite their busy lives and careers, the Trumps always made time for Sunday lunch at Mary and Fred's in Queens. She did all the cooking herself—shrimp cocktail, turkey soup, and her signature meat loaf, which is so excellent, it's served in the restaurant at the Trump Grill in Trump Tower to this day. Sometimes, the dining room conversations were impassioned and intense. Donald was very competitive with his siblings, especially Maryanne. They would try to top each other to make their points about politics and business—anything under the sun, really. As heated as their conversations could get, there was no ill will. Speaking up and shouting down was how the Trumps related to each other.

Another regular meal they shared was Wednesday dinner at Peter Luger, the legendary German steak house in Williamsburg, Brooklyn. The restaurant is rustic, with long farm tables and sawdust on the floor, and waiters dressed in black with long white aprons. We'd take over three whole tables and order porterhouses that came on sizzling-hot platters. The waiters cut the meat off the T-bone into slices, the juices pooling on one end of the platter for dipping with onion rolls. The best meat was close to the bone, but you had to pick it up and eat it with your hands. No one was going to do that at the restaurant.

One time, when the waiters were clearing the table post-meal, Donald said, "I'll take the bone in a doggie bag."

"But, Donald," I said teasingly, "we don't have a dog." He was furious. (Of course, we did have Chappy, but his family didn't know that.)

At four a.m., I found him in front of the fridge, gnawing at the bone. I couldn't blame him. It really was that good.

- 6 -

FIRST COMES MARRIAGE

In those early days in New York, I didn't know anyone, or anything about how to live there. Where could I buy groceries or toilet paper? Where should I go to get my nails done? Donald wasn't much help because he would go to work at seven a.m. and come home at seven p.m., and then we'd go out to dinner. He had no time to take me around the city and point out the important places I should know. So I spent my first month in New York exploring the city with my poodle at my side.

Donald was not a dog fan. When I told him I was bringing Chappy with me to New York, he said, "No."

"It's me and Chappy or no one!" I insisted, and that was that.

I'd put Chappy on his leash, and we'd walk around the neighborhood. He established some regular pee-pee spots, including the ivy planters outside Saint Patrick's Cathedral—a hundred-year-old Gothic Revival church where the archbishop of New York presided—on Fifth Avenue. He'd do his business, I'd cross myself, and then we'd walk on.

Chappy figured out his favorite places, but I was clueless about mine. Fortunately, I met the ultimate New York guide in the form of a five-foot-tall, razor-sharp brunette spitfire named Nikki Haskell.

I met Nikki, a socialite, TV host, diet aid entrepreneur, gossip columnist, and boldface name of the seventies and eighties, at Elaine's one night when Donald and I were having dinner there. She was seated one table over and just started talking to me, and we immediately hit it off. We've been best friends for forty years. She stays with me in Saint-Tropez and Aspen, and we still talk nearly every day. During Donald's campaign in 2016, Nikki was part of a vocal, spunky group of Bel Air women (Bill Clinton's mistress Gennifer Flowers among them) who called themselves "Trumpettes."

One of the first things Nikki said to me was "Let me see your engagement ring." I showed her. She said, "It's barely visible to the naked eye! I need a magnifying glass!" It wasn't *that* small. Another woman might've been offended, but I thought Nikki was hilarious. I could just look at her a certain way, and we'd both start cracking up. It was that kind of friendship. For years, the ring was a running joke between us. She'd say, "When are you going to upgrade that speck?" I never did because, under my layers of toughness, I do have a sentimental heart.

With my fiancé, my dog, and a new best friend, New York started to feel like home.

While Donald worked, Nikki, Chappy, and I went everywhere together, laughing and pee-peeing (one of us) all over the Upper

East Side. She introduced me to other women at La Grenouille and La Goulue during my very brief "ladies who lunch" period, when I was part of the socialite circle of women who met for grilled radicchio and shaved fennel salads to gossip and drink all day. Problem: I was never much of a drinker. A glass or two of wine with dinner is fine, but martinis in the afternoon? Not for me. Also, I couldn't stand the lateness. Like the Trumps, I am a punctual person. In those circles, being on time was the biggest waste *of* time. I'd wind up sitting at La Côte Basque, waiting for forty-five minutes for pampered housewives who didn't even have jobs. No discipline. When they finally arrived, they'd say, "The traffic was terrible!" but they lived three blocks away! I'd managed to be on time, and I had no idea where I was going.

Meanwhile, Donald and his secretary were taking care of most of the wedding plans. I didn't know who to call for the cake or the flowers or where to book the service or the reception, but Donald did. He booked the church and the '21' Club for dinner afterward. He hired the florists, and I went in to approve the arrangements. The only thing I took care of myself was the dress. I called my friend John Warren, a Canadian designer, to make my gown.

Of the six hundred people who came to my April 7, 1977, wedding at the Marble Collegiate Church on Fifth Avenue and West Twenty-Ninth Street, where the Trumps had been going for decades, I knew six of them: my girlfriends from Montreal, Nikki, my aunt, and my father. My mother wasn't feeling well and had to stay in Czechoslovakia. The wedding was the first time Donald and Dedo met. They liked and respected each other immediately, though the conversation was stilted at best: Dedo's English wasn't very good yet.

Donald and his family invited businessmen, Mayor Abe Beame, and hundreds of others. I was scared out of my mind at the idea of standing up there in my gown (white, ruched, strapless, and form-fitting), reciting my vows with my thick accent in front of all these VIPs. To make matters worse, the flowers didn't arrive! The florist called to say she was running late (do *not* get me started . . .), and I was so freaked-out with bottled-up nerves that I locked myself in the antechamber next to the chapel and cried. My father came into the room to calm me down. "You can do it, Iva," he said, using my nickname. If it weren't for Dedo's pep talk, I might never have left that room.

The florist *finally* showed up with my bouquet and we got started. My father walked me down the aisle and delivered me to Donald. Pastor Norman Vincent Peale (author of *The Power of Positive Thinking*) officiated the ceremony. The reception was at the '21' Club. Joey Adams, the comedian and husband of gossip colum-nist Cindy Adams, was the master of ceremonies. It was all a blur of smiling strangers introducing themselves and congratulating me, taking bites of food and sips of wine.

Our honeymoon in Acapulco, Mexico, lasted only two days. We had to rush back to New York so my husband could finalize the deal to buy the Commodore Hotel and convert it into the Grand Hyatt. It was a big risk for Donald, but I told him, "Take risks now when you're young, because you're not going to do it when you're older!" He proved me wrong there. Spending his own money to run for president was an even bigger risk. The biggest!

Incredibly, I got pregnant on the honeymoon. Why so incred-ible? At the time, I had an IUD implanted in my uterus. The odds of conceiving with the coil were minuscule. I always thought I was a one-in-a-million woman, but this was ridiculous. However, Donald and I were not unhappy about it. I was twenty-eight; he was thirty. We took two seconds to get over the shock and realized the pregnancy was an unexpected joy. I was going to be a mom! I was going to create a family in New York that would make my parents in Czechoslovakia proud. Family is my number one priority—always has been and always will be. I didn't know what motherhood would entail, but I knew I would handle it like everything else: with determination and confidence.

Donald and I moved to a bigger place in the Olympic Tower on East Fifty-First and Fifth Avenue, which I decorated with the passion and excitement of an expecting newlywed. Spending all my time barefoot and pregnant in my new kitchen, however? Absolutely not. I wasn't even there that often, just to sleep and have breakfast. Donald and I went out for dinner every night, and during the day, I was working full-time at my new job at a construction site.

Soon after we got back from our honeymoon, Donald had appointed me the vice president of interior design and rebranding at his new hotel. I was tasked with transforming the historic Commodore Hotel on East Forty-Second Street into the Grand Hyatt. Until then, I'd been a competitive skier, a ski instructor, and a model. Why did he make me the boss of this important project when he could have hired a dozen people with more know-how? When it came to hiring, Donald used his instincts. He knew that although I lacked experience, I had confidence, a great sense of style, unbound enthusiasm, strength, and a strong work ethic. He insisted I take the job and trusted that I could do it, so I agreed. I wasn't concerned about mixing business and family at all. Donald's was a family business, and, as a new member of the family, it made sense to put me to work.

Hit the ground running? I *broke* ground on day one.

At first, the co-owners, the Hyatt Corporation, owned by Jay Pritzker, didn't like me for the job, but Donald insisted and he got his way. Fred Trump wasn't so sure about me, either, and he kept a close eye on me. If the work fell even one day behind, he'd complain to Donald. But I stayed on top of my crews and always met my deadlines.

Every single decision, big or small—from the towels to the flooring, who to hire and fire, the completion timeline—was up to me. I would spend my day talking to marble people, drywall people, electricians, and plumbers. Taking on two huge projects—creating the aesthetic for a hotel and nurturing a human life—immediately after we'd moved and married didn't faze me. I was a natural at making quick, smart decisions. Donald told me I could go to the site whenever I wanted, and that turned out to be seven days a week. Meanwhile, he was starting the financing on our other new project, Trump Tower, and was also working constantly.

It was a heady, happy, *busy* time. To many people, starting a new job as a pregnant newlywed would be a lot. But I thrived in a high-activity atmosphere. Having so much to do, and so many responsibilities, was exhilarating. I was going a million miles a minute and felt comfortable with the pressure. My friends asked me if I felt overwhelmed. Nope. As the tornado swirled around me, I was calm at its center. I think if I had stayed at home and watched TV, I would have been climbing the walls with antsy anticipation.

Regarding pregnancy, I *hated* it! Compared to some of my

friends', my pregnancy wasn't so horrible. I didn't get morning sickness or other digestive problems. I only gained twelve pounds. Some women make pregnancy the excuse to eat ice cream non-stop. I was too busy for cravings and five meals a day. For black-tie events, I had to put aside my sexy Versace for Yves Saint Laurent sheaths that were straight columns from shoulders to hips. My feet and ankles were painfully swollen, but I stuck with my heels until the eighth month before switching to flats. Even though I wasn't vomiting or ballooning, I found pregnancy uncomfortable and wanted to get it over with as soon as possible.

When the holidays rolled around, I was increasingly worried about going into labor at work in a building without elevators, on a floor with no one but plumbers and electricians, or while traveling. Plus my hands and fingers had puffed up so much, I could barely find the diamond on my finger. (Nikki said, "Told ya.") But the holiday came and went, and the pregnancy endured. Merry Christmas? Mine was cranky.

I reached the end of my rope. I called my doctor, Robert Porges of NYU Medical Center, and said, "I can't take it anymore!"

He said, "Okay, I'll induce you. See you at the hospital at five p.m."

It was New Year's Eve, the one-year anniversary of the night Donald and I got engaged. I checked the time. It was noon; I had only five hours before I was due to report to the hospital to become a mother. I took a meeting at the hotel and then went to get a pedicure and manicure before heading home to pack an overnight bag. At five p.m. on the dot, Donald and I were in the hospital room, and I was ready to go.

Dr. Porges came in with a needle full of a drug that would

start my contractions. He said, "It might take some time before it works."

Two minutes later, I had my first contraction, and then one after another, without a break between them. There was no chance to give me an epidural. People always say that you forget the pain, but I will never forget it! My back was killing me, and they gave me a pill for that, but it was brutal nonetheless.

Ten minutes later, it was time to push.

I kicked Donald out of the room. Let him witness the birth? Never. My sex life would be finished after that. I know some people videotape their children's births, but I didn't even want the nurses to see mine. I threw everyone out of the room. This was between me and my doctor.

He said, "Push!"

I know my body well from being an athlete, so I contracted all the right muscles. I think other women bear down in the wrong places, like their earlobes or necks or cheeks. I put my energy where it counted. Ten minutes later, my son was born. The clock on the wall said five twenty p.m. Start to finish, my entire labor and delivery lasted twenty minutes. I love speed in skiing, driving, and giving birth, but that was *really* fast, even for me—but not too fast. Twenty minutes was plenty of time to experience the pain and satisfaction of giving birth. It would be the same for each baby: a horrible, mercifully brief, and beautiful experience.

The nurses were allowed to come back in and take care of the baby while Dr. Porges sewed me up. (I had to sit on an inner tube for a week because of those stitches.) Only after the doctor finished sewing was Donald permitted into the room again, and we held our baby for the first time. He was adorable, warm, perfect, with dark Zelnicek eyes. I saw my father in him, my mother, and my husband, too. I'd hated pregnancy, but I loved the end result.

Donald said, "What should we name him?"

"Donald Junior," I said.

"You can't do that!"

"Why not?"

"What if he's a loser?"

"I carried him for nine months. I get to decide on the name! He's Donald."

We took turns holding him, and talked about the things we'd do and what a fabulous, happy life he was going to have. We also talked a little business. Even in those first hours of being new parents, we couldn't help ourselves. The business mind ran in the blood. As I said, I got mine from my grandmother Katrine, and it blossomed in my marriage with Donald. I was sure that little Don had it in him, too.

I felt bad that I was keeping Dr. Porges from his New Year's Eve party, so I sent him home. Donald stayed until eight p.m., and then I sent him home, too. Nikki stopped by with champagne, and then she had a party to go to. I knew one of my girlfriends was on another floor of the hospital recovering from back surgery, so around ten p.m., after the nurses took Don into the nursery to sleep, I put a boa and my mink over my nightgown and went to visit her. My friend and I rang in the New Year together, and then I went back to my room.

A medical student rushed in, looking panicked, and said, "I'm looking for Mrs. Trump."

"That's me."

He looked me up and down and said, "You can't be Mrs. Trump. She gave birth a few hours ago." I found out that they thought I'd been kidnapped! The staff had been frantically searching all over the hospital for me.

My employees at the Grand Hyatt were thrilled to hear that I'd given birth to Don over the weekend. I'd been tough on them about deadlines, and apparently some of them liked the idea that I'd be out of commission for a month postpartum. On Monday, January 2, I greeted the workmen at the hotel by saying, "I'm back! Did you miss me?"

I didn't breastfeed any of my children, not because I have anything against it. I just couldn't imagine having a kid clamped to my chest for hours a day. It didn't mesh with my work schedule. People said, "You could pump the milk." Forget it. Besides the fact that hooking up a machine to the nipples is totally unsexy, how would I manage it? Go into a construction site Port-A-John to pump my breasts every three hours? No. Formula was fine. All of my children grew healthy and tall on it.

For birth control, I considered going on the Pill, but I knew I'd forget to take it at the same time every day. With some misgivings, I had another IUD put in. Three years later, the same thing happened! I got pregnant with Ivanka despite having the device. We named our second bundle of unexpected joy Ivana after me and called her Ivanka, which translates as "little Ivana." Everyone assumes her nickname is her given name. Donald floated the idea of naming her Tiffany because he'd just bought the air rights over Tiffany & Co., the jewelry store on Fifth Avenue next to Trump Tower. I vetoed that. He had Don, and I had Ivanka.

A new IUD went in, and the doctors swore up and down it was going to work this time. "Ivana, *you will not get pregnant!*" they said.

A year and a half later, Eric was conceived.

Donald and I had a cottage in East Hampton by Georgica Pond for summer weekends. It was a beautiful house, a haven, and it always smelled like roses. If the ocean was calm, I'd take Don and Ivanka to the beach to swim. They'd spend hours playing with their toys in the sand, digging and building castles. If the ocean was too rough, they'd play by the pond, catching frogs and sailing toy boats. I cultivated a vegetable garden and coaxed tomatoes, cucumbers, and carrots out of the ground. We'd have so many tomatoes at the end of the summer, I couldn't give them away fast enough—and, believe me, I tried. Don and Ivanka had their own bedrooms, and so did my parents, who came to stay with us all summer long. My father played with the kids, and my mother cooked dinners using the vegetables from my garden. I have many happy memories with the kids in the Hamptons. We'd go biking and strawberry picking, and buy fresh corn and potatoes from farmers markets and then put them on the grill along with steak and lobsters for Sunday barbecue lunches.

We had a dune buggy. I'm crazy about speed and would tear around the beach, jumping dunes, catching air. I took out the buggy when I was four months pregnant with Eric on one of the last days of summer. I might've taken some jumps that were higher, and spins that were faster, than I should have. I rode home and handed off the buggy to Donald for his last ride of the summer. I went to change out of my beach clothes, and I saw blood in my shorts. My heart leapt into my throat and I thought, *I'm losing the baby.*

This was before cell phones, so I couldn't just call Donald to come home. I ran next door to my friend and future lawyer Michael Kennedy's house and said, "Take me to the emergency room!" The traffic on the main streets was horrible, but Michael knew all the back roads and got me to the hospital as soon as possible.

I stayed in Southampton Hospital for two days until the doctors were sure that I wasn't going to miscarry. Obviously, Eric survived, and I didn't do him any damage, but I sure beat myself up about being reckless. It was stupid to ride the buggy that day. I should have known better. I'd put my body through much worse as a skier, and I thought I could handle it. It was a wake-up call, a reminder that my body wasn't only my own for the next few months.

Eric knows this story, and he uses it as ammunition when he says I didn't really want him. I assure him that it's true the pregnancy wasn't planned, but when I saw the blood and felt the terror that I might lose him, it made me love him even more, which is absolutely true.

Becoming a mother changed me in so many ways. I had not only babies to share my life with but also a clear mission for what it would be about: protecting and loving my children the way my parents had protected and loved me. I was responsible for everything they'd learn, for instilling admirable values, and for providing them with the kind of security I didn't have when I was young. I had all the love in the world. My children would have that, as well as security, comfort, and freedom.

After Eric's arrival, our family was complete. My doctor asked if I wanted to do the IUD again.

I said, "Have you lost your *mind*?"

I had my tubes tied instead. I was thirty-five. I'd had three babies in six years and that was enough. The store was closed.

—————————— DON ——————————

Birth-order dynamics are interesting to think about. The standard line is that firstborns are reliable achievers, middle kids are extroverted rebels, and last-borns are fun-loving and self-centered. That doesn't work perfectly for our family. As they say, "Self-praise is no recommendation," but I have been told that I was always a very protective person. I guess I was very protective of Ivanka, and although Eric was six years younger, he always seemed to be beside me or behind me. He was always, always there! So, as a firstborn, I would say I was maybe reliable. But in some ways, I was the most rebellious of the three of us. Ivanka was a middle child, but I wouldn't describe her as an extroverted rebel! Perhaps gently extroverted, but rebel in the second-child sense of the word? No. Last-born Eric is fun-loving, yes, but self-centered? Absolutely *not*. Eric doesn't have a bad bone in his body.

When Don was an infant, we lived at Olympic Towers in a two-bedroom apartment. Donald and I slept in one room. Don and the Swiss nanny slept in the other. I was terrified of sudden infant death syndrome (we called it "crib death" back then) and would creep into the nursery in the middle of the night to make sure he was still breathing. I was also scared of the strict Swiss nanny. She kept Don on a sleep schedule and if I woke him accidentally, she'd get mad at me and accuse me of not trusting her. But if I didn't check on my son, I'd lie awake in bed, fretting myself into a state.

After a month, I got rid of the Swiss nanny and hired Trudy. She was German, young, and very sweet. She knew a lot about babies and children from helping her mother raise her ten brothers and sisters. Trudy stayed with us after we moved again, to the penthouse of 800 Fifth Avenue. One time, I came home to an empty apartment—no Trudy, no Chappy. I searched the place and found one-year-old Don in the bathtub by himself. The nanny had gone outside to walk the dog and left my son waist-deep in hot water. Of course, I freaked out, and screamed at her when she got back. Once she realized what she had done, she apologized, cried, and swore she'd never make that mistake again.

I'm a big believer in second chances. We all screw up sometimes. I decided to forgive her and let her keep her job. And she did keep her promise never to make *that* mistake again. But she made an even bigger one.

Trudy grew up in a huge family with not a lot of money, so her mother used to make a big pot of chicken soup every week. Trudy didn't know how to cook in smaller amounts, so she'd make her mother's three-chickens-in-a-pot recipe. She put two-year-old Don on the kitchen counter while she chopped the carrots and onions so she could keep an eye on him. She looked away for a minute, and Don fell off the counter, breaking his leg. We rushed him to the hospital, and the doctors put a plaster cast on his leg from knee to toes. When Donald found out, he was furious.

And still I didn't fire her! I thought about it, and Trudy was terrified that I would. But in the end, I couldn't bring myself to do it. She was a good person, very loving and caring, sweet, if not too smart. She was only human, and mistakes do happen. It could have happened with me, and it might one day. The broken leg wasn't life threatening. I felt sorry for her. She needed the job and we liked her, so I convinced Donald that she'd learned her lesson (again) and should stay. In hindsight, I probably should have fired her.

Trudy worked for our family for five years, through Don's toddlerhood and Ivanka's infancy. By the time Eric arrived in January 1984, we'd moved into the thirty-thousand-square-foot penthouse on the top three floors of Trump Tower. I'd been in charge of the interiors there, too, from the lobby, with its famous fountain, to every room in our triplex.

Our last move felt like a fresh start and a natural break. I let Trudy go, and I signed up with another agency to find her replacement. A woman named Bridget Carroll came for an interview. She was Irish, older, a religious Catholic, had been a nanny for John Kennedy Jr., and had excellent recommendations. She struck me as a salt-of-the-earth, good-hearted person . . . and I struck her as a terrifying ogre. I have no idea why she was so scared of me. If I walked down the hall toward her, she'd cower against the wall. Whenever I spoke to her, she stared at her feet. I didn't care how she felt about me as long as she loved the kids and they loved her. Bridget came into our lives when Ivanka was just starting to walk, and the two of them bonded instantly. My daughter was easy to love. She never cried, never fussed, just sunshine and light, smiles and giggles. Bridget doted on her, as Donald and I did, too.

Since Bridget couldn't work, and shouldn't have worked, seven days a week, we called the agency back and they sent us Dorothy Curry to share the responsibilities. Dorothy was also Irish and religious, much younger than Bridget, with a sparkle in her eye and plenty of nervous energy. Eric became "her" baby, and they formed a special relationship and a closeness that they still share to this day.

(Once the kids had all grown up, Dorothy transitioned to a new role in our family as my personal assistant. She continues to work for me to this day, thirty-two years after we first met.)

Bridget would work for two days, and then Dorothy took over for two. When they were "on," they slept in a lovely room off the kitchen on the kids' floor in the triplex. When they were "off," they went back to their own apartments. The arrangement worked out beautifully. We were finally settled in our permanent home, with the support of two wonderful women who became like family. For me, the move into Trump Tower and hiring Bridget and Dorothy were like putting the final puzzle pieces in place, allowing the big picture of my new life as a wife, mother, and businesswoman to become clear.

ERIC

Dorothy is my second mother. She's raised me since I was a baby, and we are incredibly close—inseparable. I love her immensely. She's a big, and very important, part of our family.

Dorothy is originally from Ireland, and during the summer she would take me there for a week or two. She is from Belturbet, a little town in County Cavan. Dorothy has a number of sisters, and we stayed at their houses. Even when Dorothy wasn't working, she was still with me. We traveled all over Ireland and saw all the castles. Northern Ireland had a rough political climate back then. While traveling, we had to pass through security checkpoints. Men with machine guns would demand to see our passports, but I always felt safe with Dorothy.

Obviously, a lot's changed. A couple of years ago, the Trump Organization bought a hotel on the west coast of Ireland called Doonbeg, about forty minutes outside Shannon. It's a beautiful place that brings me back to Dorothy in a certain way. I may not be Irish by blood, but I feel like part of me is Irish in my upbringing because of her presence.

PART THREE

BRINGING UP TRUMP

7

SNAPSHOT

When I was seventeen, I slept in a crawl space in our small house in Zlín. By the time I was thirty-five, I lived in a penthouse in Trump Tower on Fifth Avenue. There were many steps and stages along the way: my student life in Prague and modest house in Montreal. Donald's and my first three apartments in New York were fine but not what anyone would call extravagant. The change in my life circumstances took place over fifteen years, and it was a gradual rise. I didn't wake up rich. I worked extremely hard throughout my life and became wealthy because of my work ethic and energy. That, and because my partner in business and life had the same ambition that I did. I never set out to be wealthy or to marry a rich man. When I met Donald, he wasn't superrich, but he had big dreams.

We both worked nonstop to realize them, and moving into Trump Tower with our three babies felt like the culmination of that dream. Along the way, there wasn't a lot of time to reflect on how far we'd come. I knew I was incredibly fortunate to have a wonderful husband, healthy children, and a career that suited me perfectly. Living in a beautiful home was icing on the cake.

So what was it like to live in Trump Tower? Let me paint the picture.

A SNAPSHOT OF OUR HOME

Without question, we lived in the lap of luxury. I pulled out all the stops while decorating the Trump Tower triplex. If something could be leafed in gold or upholstered with damask, it was. Italian marble? I bought a mountain's worth. Cream-and-rust-colored onyx floors and a thousand-crystal chandelier? Why not? It was the eighties, and my aesthetic at the time was over-the-top glitz, glamour, and drama. My goal was to shock and amaze my guests when they walked into the space.

The sixty-eighth floor was known as "the kids' floor," with their bedrooms, an entertainment room, the nannies' room, a kitchen, and two suites, one for my parents and one for guests. I let the kids decorate their own spaces. I had final approval—I wouldn't allow posters of creepy rockers or half-naked supermodels on the walls—but the kids were otherwise free to do what they wanted. Eric chose yellow and white walls, with shelves full of his toys and books. Ivanka's room was lilac and mint green with a wrought-iron bed and frilly canopy, Bon Jovi and *Beverly Hills, 90210* posters on the walls, and floor-to-ceiling windows overlooking Central Park. Donny chose very simple, nautical colors of blue and white, and covered his walls with movie, sports, and band posters. I don't think Don really cared at all about his room—it was just the place where he slept and dressed and waited to go back outside.

The entertainment room was filled with toys, rocking horses, Matchbox cars, Tonka trucks, puzzles and games, books, and enormous bins full of Lincoln Logs and Legos. The boys and Ivanka made forts with couch cushions and blankets. Although she had dozens of dolls to choose from, Ivanka wasn't that interested in "girl" toys. She preferred to do whatever her brothers were up to, and if that meant building racetracks out of blocks for the Matchbox cars, that's what she did. Even though he was the oldest, Don didn't boss his siblings around. Since they liked the same toys, they played happily as a unit at whatever game was decided on for that afternoon. They had a big-screen TV and a VHS player. Ivanka's all-time favorite movie was *The Sound of Music*. She played that video ten times a week, sang along, and danced on the furniture. Don preferred PG-rated action shows like *The A-Team* and *MacGyver*. When Eric was little, he loved *Pee-wee's Playhouse*. You could hear him laughing from the other side of the floor.

I had a humidity-and-temperature-controlled fur vault for my dozens of designer mink, sable, and chinchilla coats. The kids would break into it and pull my furs off the hangers to use in their games. I remember coming home once and finding my furs turned into tee-pees in the entertainment room. Chappy raided the fur closet, too, and turned my chinchilla into the world's most expensive dog bed.

A SNAPSHOT OF THE ROUTINE

At home, our lives were planned on an intentional routine. I was our family's supreme leader and set rules that no one ever questioned. Our weekdays ran like clockwork. It's possible the kids hankered for spontaneity in their heart of hearts, but they didn't dare complain to me about their rigid schedule. It was the law, like the Constitution or the Ten Commandments, and the kids knew never to break it.

At six thirty a.m., we woke up and got dressed. At seven a.m., we had a breakfast of cereal, fruit, and yogurt, and we always ate together. Then the nannies or I would take the kids down to the twenty-eighth floor to visit Donald at the Trump Organization office for a morning hello before walking them to their schools nearby. I went to work and I would pick them up at school if possible (if I couldn't make it, the nannies did). Then we'd take them to Central Park to run around for an hour or two to get sun and fresh air, or they'd go with the nannies to after-school activities. Around four thirty p.m., the kids would stop again in Donald's office to play on the carpet with the toys he kept there for them.

At five p.m., everyone (except Donald) was back home for the kids' dinner hour. I'd sit with my children while they ate, and we'd talk about their day. I asked typical mom questions, like "What did you learn today?" or, to Ivanka, "How was ballet?" Then they'd do their homework, and if they had time left over, the kids were allowed to watch TV or play games before a bath, a story, and bed at seven p.m. There was no discussion about bedtime. It might seem early, but they were exhausted. I grew up on an early-bird schedule and managed to pack a lot of activity into my day, too. After the kids were in bed for the night, Donald and I would go out for dinner, or to a club or an event (schmoozing was a big part of the real estate business; for me, it was an extension of the workday). Sometimes, Donald and I stayed in to watch *Dynasty* and *Dallas*.

The fact that every minute of their lives was planned gave me a sense of comfort and security. I could be walking through a construction site or in a meeting with my vice presidents, look down at my watch, and know exactly what each of my children was doing at that second. It also allowed me to spend as much time with them as possible in the mornings and evenings. It was for their benefit, too. Because the kids were kept busy and on a tight schedule, they didn't have time to get into trouble.

The weekends were more relaxed. The official start to every weekend was when the kids burst into our bedroom, screaming, to take flying leaps onto our bed. It was enormous, an Alaska king that could have qualified for its own zip code. I know it was a crazy extravagance, but I loved that bed! The kids considered it their personal bouncy castle. Chappy got riled up from all the excitement, barking and wagging his tail. I'd get out of bed and take Chappy up the staircase to the roof for a quick pee-pee. The roof was bordered on all sides by a high wall, so it was safe up there for him and the kids to get some fresh air if they didn't want to go all the way down to the street. Weekends were for family time, usually spent in the country. It was our chance to let the kids go crazy on bikes or just roam around the yard. If we had outings planned, we were always on time, but I tried to keep the weekend schedule a bit loose. Everyone needs unstructured time to let the imagination run wild.

Regardless of the day of the week, the last thing the kids did before sleep was to say their prayers. I didn't have organized religion growing up because of the communists, though my parents were Catholics and, as a family, we prayed secretly at home. When I first came to America, Donald and I went to midnight Mass at Saint Patrick's Cathedral (for me) and Protestant Sunday services at Marble Collegiate (for him). I wanted my children to have a grounding in faith. I didn't know the prayers in English, so the nannies, devoted Irish Catholics, taught the kids what to say. Bridget was a three-times-a-week churchgoer and knew all the words by heart. Every night, Bridget and Dorothy would kneel by the side of the kids' beds and say the lines for them to repeat. I can't say that religion plays a large role in my life now, but I'm glad the children grew up talking to God and having something to believe in.

A SNAPSHOT OF THEIR STYLE

When they weren't in school uniforms, the kids dressed in whatever they liked on Saturdays and Sundays, which was usually jeans, T-shirts, and Adidas sneakers. Style wasn't a major concern when they were young. Ivanka liked velvet-and-lace party dresses and patent-leather Mary Janes, but the boys couldn't have cared less what they wore.

I was the hairstylist for the family. Once a month, when the boys' hair got too shaggy, I'd make Don and Eric sit down on a chair, tie a towel around their necks, place a figurative bowl on their heads, and trim the strands that peeked out from under it. It took all of five minutes, which was, for them, an eternity of sitting still.

As soon as I said, "Okay, you're done," they'd run around the room with the towel on like a Superman cape while I screamed at them not to get the hair trimmings all over the house.

Ivanka's hair got the at-home treatment, too, but she was spared the bowl. I just trimmed the dead ends. Although a Dorothy Hamill wedge would have been cute on her, she and I liked her hair princess length. I have fond memories of my mother brushing and braiding my hair as a little girl, and I hope Ivanka remembers my doing that for her. At parties and for photos, I pulled her hair away from her face with ribbons and bows to match her white ruffled Bonpoint dresses. I loved indulging her in the "girly" things we both loved so much.

IVANKA

My parents went out nearly every night. After we had dinner and I had a bath, I'd get in my pajamas and would spend forty-five minutes with Mom in her large beautiful bathroom as she got ready. Her bathroom was on the sixty-seventh floor of Trump Tower and had a wall of windows with incredible views overlooking the city skyline. I'd sit on the edge of the tub and watch her get dressed and do her makeup.

Nowadays, going out in New York can be casual. But back then, in the eighties, things were more formal, either cocktail or black-tie. She'd go into her huge closet and pick out what she was going to wear, and then I'd help her zip up the back of her dress. We'd sit side by side at the mirror while she did her makeup. I'd put on her red lipstick while she did her blue eye shadow. Sometimes, I'd have to take a second bath because I looked like a clown with all her makeup on my face. No matter where she was going or how much of a hurry she was in, she always tucked me in on her way out the door.

AN ACTUAL SNAPSHOT OF THEIR LIVES

When Don was eight, Ivanka four, and Eric two, I met a woman named Jill Krementz at a party, who said to me, "I'm a freelance photographer, and I'd like to take a photo of your kids." We'd done formal photo shoots with the whole family, including a famous portrait of the five of us posing on the white spiral staircase in the triplex, all of us dressed in red and black. But I liked Jill's idea of doing a series of casual, candid shots of the kids at play, like a wildlife photographer catching animals and birds in their natural habitat.

So one afternoon, the kids wore their T-shirts and jeans and trooped off to Central Park with the nannies after school as usual. Jill came to the playground and just started shooting them from behind a tree, as inconspicuously as possible. The kids didn't even know she was there for most of it.

I showed up at one point and observed the whole scene. The nannies were watching the kids. The security men were watching the kids. The photographer was shooting the kids. I was watching the nannies, the bodyguards, the photographer, and the kids. The children themselves were rolling in the grass, chasing each other, and having the time of their lives.

Just like I had been throughout my childhood, my kids were being watched, but their watchers had only the best of intentions. It was a grateful moment for me. I'd managed to give my children the same discipline and structure that my parents gave me, minus the anxiety and fear. When Jill asked me to pose for a few pictures with the kids, I was all smiles

8

MINOR CRIME AND PUNISHMENT

Don got in trouble with me more often than the other kids, probably because he was the oldest. Ivanka and Eric would see me punish him, and they learned not to make his mistakes. One time, we were having a dinner with the Trump clan at Gurney's, a famous resort and spa in Montauk. It was a special occasion, a celebration, and we were dressed up. Don wore a suit and looked very handsome. Ivanka was in one of her cute white dresses. Eric was just a baby but also in a tiny suit with a little tie.

You'll never guess what the Trumps ordered for their entrées.

Anyway, the dinner was going on . . . and on. I sympathized with the kids, having to sit still for so long. I felt the same way, but when you're out to dinner with the family, especially the Trumps, who expected children not to distract from the adult conversation, you behave.

Nowadays, nothing annoys me more than little kids screaming and running around when I'm trying to have a quiet meal with good food, wine, and conversation. The parents just smile, shrug, and say, "Kids will be kids." At McDonald's, kids can be kids. But not at upscale restaurants! Parents shouldn't bring kids to nice restaurants in the first place, but if they do and can't get them under control, they should leave.

At the Gurney's dinner, Don started to act silly. He was making faces and playing with the butter, clanging his forks and spoons together, giggling. Everyone, including my father-in-law, looked at him disapprovingly.

I said, "Don, let's go to the bathroom."

I took him to an empty hallway and said, "If you don't stop acting up, you're going to get spanked!" I swatted him a few times on his behind just so he knew I was serious, and we went back to the table. He sat in his chair and didn't dare cry in front of the whole family. It was obvious he'd just been punished. I could tell he was struggling to keep his chin under control. But he did, and he behaved for the rest of the night, and for every long dinner to come.

––––––––––––––––––––––– ERIC –––––––––––––––––––––––

Mom was not afraid to spank. If one of us messed up, he or she was punished, so we learned to behave. None of us have attitudes or egos. If we showed any hint of that or talked back, we'd be on the receiving end of her anger and disappointment.

She kept us in line, and she also gave us a lot of latitude. We went to R-rated movies, boxing matches, and concerts, as the only kids in the room. She wasn't a soccer-mom type with an ever-ready bottle of Purell who chases down her kid because he touched a worm.

New Yorkers talk about traffic like war stories. At coffee or dinner with friends, they say, "Oh my God! The traffic back to Manhattan from the Hamptons on Sunday was *a nightmare!*" and everyone leans in to hear about it because they know they'll get their turn to tell their own bumper-to-bumper horror story. The only antidote to traffic hell is bitching about it.

It goes without saying that traffic on the way home from your weekend house is a good problem to have. But it was still a huge pain in the ass. The Long Island "Distressway" on Sunday was like a parking lot. If you left at three p.m. after a barbecue lunch, you got slammed at Exit 56 by Jones Beach. If you left at six p.m., you got crushed right out of the gate. If you left at eight p.m., you stopped dead as soon as you crossed the bridge into Manhattan. If you left at eleven p.m., you wouldn't get home until one a.m., which ruined the next day. But if you got up early and left on Monday at five a.m., you got stuck between fish and vegetable trucks the whole ride into the city.

We were fortunate to have a problem like this, but Donald and I *hated* it anyway. Sunday traffic wiped out the good feeling of a fun weekend. We talked about taking the helicopter to and from, but that was over-the-top, even for us. It says a lot about just how awful the traffic was that we decided to sell the cottage and buy a new weekend/summer house in Greenwich, Connecticut, only thirty-odd miles from Manhattan. It'd be a much shorter commute, about forty-five minutes from door to door.

I hired a real estate broker and we flew around the area in the helicopter so she could point out the estates that were available and tell me a bit about them. (I know how crazy that sounds. At times, I'd stop and think, *I have a helicopter*, and feel amazed at life's twists and turns. I never took anything for granted, especially not our homes.) I'd get an aerial view and decide which ones to visit. I picked a mansion that was close to the Boat & Yacht Club and Manero's Restaurant, with seventeen bedrooms, a dining room with a table that sat twenty, a living room as spacious as a barn, a solarium, a breakfast room, three large kitchens, a playroom for the kids, a ten-car garage, and a bowling alley in the basement.

──────────────────── IVANKA ────────────────────

Manero's was a steak house in Greenwich, Connecticut, where we had a lot of family meals. We'd all order the same thing: steak and a big Caesar salad to share. I'd order a giant baked potato with massive amounts of sour cream, an unhealthy, ridiculous amount, like a whole pint just for me. That was my go-to order. It was a loud, busy place with waiters who sang "Happy Birthday," very family friendly at a time when most restaurants didn't do that. They were so into the bring-the-kids attitude that they had a sign on the wall that said, "If you deliver a baby at Manero's, your whole family eats for free for the rest of your life!" or something like that. I would beg Mom to have another baby just so I could order those baked potatoes forever.

I decorated the entire house, choosing every carpet, strip of wallpaper, piece of art, stick of furniture, and light fixture. Although the inside was gorgeous, the best thing about the property was its water borders on three sides—on one side, the Long Island Sound, and on the other two, a large pond. We also had an expansive deck overlooking the sound, and a dock for the speedboat. The boys spent more time on or around the water—boating, fishing with my father, swimming—than in the house itself.

On Friday afternoons, the nannies, kids, dog, and parakeet would pile into the back of the limo, and I'd get behind the wheel to drive to Greenwich. I felt like a bus driver. Driving a limo isn't that hard. It's just longer, so you have to make wider turns on Park Avenue. Other drivers on the highway would always take a peek as the limo went past. It's only natural. When they noticed that Ivana Trump was driving, the other drivers did a hilarious double take. I'm surprised I didn't cause any car accidents. Sunday traffic hell back to the city? It was completely avoided. Donald would take the sports car back early Monday morning before the highway got congested. If the kids had school, the nannies would ride in the limo with a driver. I'd take the seaplane right from our dock to Atlantic City to the Trump Plaza Hotel and Casino and later to Trump Castle, where I was working at the time.

One weekend, I was stuck in Atlantic City until Saturday morning and flew in by seaplane alone. I always loved the final stretch of the ride to the house. The property would come into view slowly, and I could look directly into the glass-walled breakfast room to get a perfect view of my favorite chandeliers, a pair of identical Meissen porcelain beauties.

That day, through the seaplane windows, I noticed that the kids were in there. They had their own breakfast room that was infinitely more kid friendly, and the rule was that they weren't supposed to go in the glass-walled room at all, let alone play there. As soon as I reached the dock, I jumped out and ran up to the French doors, and saw what was really going on. All three of them were scurrying around, picking up pieces of something on the table and the floor.

I looked up. One of the chandeliers had been shattered.

I must have screamed. The kids stopped moving and just stared at me, like deer in headlights.

"What happened?" I asked.

Eight-year-old Don explained that they were playing with a tennis ball, and it bounced off the table and hit the chandelier, breaking one of the china arms, which crashed down and broke into a thousand pieces.

"Who did it?" I was furious.

Ivanka, four, said, "Donny!"

I grabbed him and spanked the hell out of him. The whole time, he was saying, "It wasn't me!"

I eventually found out the truth from Dorothy. Don *was* innocent. The real culprit was . . . Ivanka! She always wanted to play with the boys and prove she was as strong as they were, so she threw the tennis ball too hard. Even while her brother took the punishment for her crime, she didn't admit her guilt, and Don didn't tell on his sister.

I felt bad I'd spanked the wrong kid, but what could I do about it then? Spank Ivanka? My anger was gone already. Apologize to Don? Then he wouldn't be the hero for his sister anymore. I let it go. Secretly, I was proud of him, and gave him extra love and ice cream for the rest of the weekend. For Ivanka's part, her own guilt was punishment enough. She never blamed her brothers for something she did again (that I know of . . .).

The children were very well behaved. I wasn't worried at all that they'd rebel when they hit adolescence because I kept them on a short leash as teenagers, too.

Ivanka likes to tell the story about the time she and some of her high school friends went to get their belly buttons pierced, and she had to decide on the spot whether to do it or not. She has said that, at the critical moment, she thought of how her father and I would react and didn't do it. Good choice! If she'd come home with a nose or belly button piercing, a tattoo, or a shaved head, I would have killed her.

--- IVANKA ---

During my punk phase in the nineties, I was really into Nirvana. My wardrobe consisted of ripped corduroy jeans and flannel shirts. One day after school, I dyed my hair blue. Mom wasn't a fan of this decision. She took one look at me and immediately went out to the nearest drugstore to buy a $10 box of Nice'n Easy. That night, she forced me to dye my hair back to blond. The color she picked out was actually three shades lighter than my natural color . . . and I have never looked back!

It wasn't too long after this that Kurt Cobain, the singer, songwriter, and guitarist for Nirvana, committed suicide. It was a shock and I was distraught. Mom had no idea who Kurt Cobain was, and she sympathized only so much. After twenty-four hours of my crying inconsolably in my room, alone—major melodrama—Mom had to pull me out of there to go down to dinner.

When they were fifteen or so, the kids started to go out with friends at night. I gave them an early curfew of ten p.m. Ivanka made a case for pushing it to midnight, saying all her friends got to stay out late and that being the first to leave was hurting her social life.

That didn't move me one inch. The real trouble with teenagers started *after* ten o'clock and I made sure my kids were home safe by then. And if they stayed out past curfew, they knew what it meant: *grounded for life!*

Over my dead body would Ivanka be like many of my friends' kids, going to discos and staying out until four a.m. Those girls, and many of their one-tenth-of-the-one-percent contemporaries, had stacks of hundreds in their wallets and loose or no curfews. Of course they went to clubs, bought bottles of Cristal and Grey Goose, and took car services home at dawn. My kids didn't have any money to blow on clubs, drugs, or car services. If you give kids money and cut them slack about bending the rules, it ruins them. I saw this in countless rich families around us in New York. Parents were lax about discipline, and the kids took advantage of it. Friends of mine would call me and complain that their child threw a party when they were away for the weekend and trashed the place. If I even so much as suspected my kids were sneaking around behind my back, breaking the rules, or lying to me, I would have been furious. They wouldn't have dared. Following my rules was so internalized by then, it was automatic. A loud voice inside their brains yelled, "Do what Mom says, *or else!*" They knew I'd be waiting by the door at ten p.m. or that my spies—the nannies and security guards—would report back to me exactly when the kids got home. An early curfew for all three meant that they'd be home at ten p.m. together. While their friends were partying and doing drugs, mine were forming sibling bonds that are just as strong today as they were twenty-five years ago.

IVANKA

I know my mother thinks I never broke the rules or did anything she wouldn't approve of, but there were many times during my teenage years when I pushed the envelope and would test the boundaries. My parents were strict, but there was still room to rebel like any other teenager.

I *am* shocked! I want to know exactly what she . . . actually, I don't. She slipped some things by me? Fine. But whatever she did, it wasn't so bad that she was arrested, or that we had to bail her out of jail, or that something awful was posted on the Internet that can't be unseen. They steered away from risky behavior that would damage them or embarrass their parents. If anyone in our family showed up in the gossip columns for going to a wild party, it would be me.

9

THE COMPETITIVE EDGE

Sports were a huge part of my childhood. As a teenager, skiing took me around the world and showed me a different way of life than I could have imagined otherwise. It also taught me how to face my fears, push myself to victory, and be humble in defeat—all lessons the kids needed to learn.

As soon as they could stand, I put them on skis. Ivanka and Don loved it from day one. They had no fear because they were only three feet tall. If they fell, it wasn't far to the ground. Eric hated skiing at first. I remember one time, in the middle of summer when he was three, he said, totally out of the blue at breakfast, "I don't want to go to Aspen. I don't want to ski."

I said, "You *will* go to Aspen, and you *will* ski."

Discussion over.

My instincts told me that Eric would love it once he got better at it, and the only way to improve was to do it, so I made him persevere. I didn't expect any of the kids to devote themselves to skiing the way I did or to practice eight hours a day. To them, it was a fun activity for us to do together. I saw it as much more than that.

In life and sports, you have to learn how to play, and win, by *doing*. The best lesson I could ever teach my kids was that you have to set a goal for yourself and work as hard as you can to achieve it. I never made it to the Olympics, but I got damn close. I'm proud of my record as an athlete. Playing sports gives you the desire to be the best. If you develop a competitive drive early in life, it'll stay with you for forever.

ERIC

We spent practically every Christmas skiing out in Colorado. Obviously, my mom was an amazing skier. She put me on skis when I could barely walk and dropped me at a ski school called Powder Pandas. I wanted nothing to do with it at the time. It was cold. I was miserable. I didn't get it, and I didn't like being separated from the adults. She would promise to buy me an apple pie at McDonald's afterward if I got through the whole day. I loved those, so I hung in there.

We went back the following year and the year after that, and I became a good skier. I "graduated" from Powder Pandas when I was four or five, and then went over to Aspen Mountain and was expected to keep up with the big boys and girls. In the Trump family, there wasn't a whole lot of waiting around. You had to fend for yourself. We skied in order, with my mom in front, followed by Don, then Ivanka, and then me. I'd be totally out of control in the back trying to keep up. I had to rise to the occasion. I'd see the others walking to the gondola and I'd have to run with all my equipment to catch them. I certainly broke a lot of goggles learning how to ski that way, but I also got really good, really fast. And once I got the hang of it, I loved it.

On a typical Aspen vacation morning, I would hit the black-diamond expert slopes on one side of the mountain. In the afternoon when Donald was making calls, I joined Don, Ivanka, and Eric on the bunny slope with Rick, their instructor. On the lift, the kids whined about how cold and tired they were. They glanced at each other, and then Don spoke for all of them, saying, "We don't want to ski anymore today."

Aspen in December could hit twenty below. I was *always* cold in my thin ski pants with Hanes panty hose underneath, socks, a turtleneck sweater, a slim-fitting jacket, and a furry Cossack hat. The kids, meanwhile, wore five layers of goose down, double gloves, double socks, and big pom-pom hats. I would just look at them to feel warmer. If I could take it in my outfit, they would ski for one more hour in theirs.

I said, "Okay. You don't have to ski, but that means Rick won't get paid today. He won't have money to buy dinner for his two kids. If you want his children to have food on the table, keep skiing. But if you don't care if they go hungry tonight, we can quit right now."

"No!" They looked horrified.

"Are you sure?"

"Yes!"

We stayed on the slope for another hour. Once quitting was no longer an option, they had a great time. It was Aspen on a sunny day! What's not to love?

For the record, I had no idea if Rick even had kids, and he got paid for the day regardless of when we stopped.

I had my reasons for pushing them so hard. If you quit at the first twinge of discomfort, you become weak. But if you exercise your endurance muscle, you grow strong. All those times I forced them to keep going added up. Look at what they endure now as public figures and business leaders. Would they have the strength to keep going today if I hadn't taught them to ignore minor discomfort—"It's cold!" "My boots hurt!" "I'm tired!"—back then? By enduring, they learned just how good it feels to push past preconceived limits.

I encouraged their competitive edge *and* sibling rivalry on the slopes by setting challenges for them. Who can get to the gondola fastest? Who can make the sharpest turns? I didn't have to do much. The kids wanted to see who was the best. Donald would race against them, too. One time, Donald was slightly behind Ivanka, and he reached out, grabbed her pole, and pulled her back so that he could glide ahead and win the race. Ivanka didn't get mad about it. She set out to beat him the next time.

The Kennedy family was always in Aspen at the same time as the Trumps, and we'd have side-by-side slalom races against them. It was Trump vs. Kennedy, and Trump always won. They were good sports about it and we always had fun with them. For the Trumps, the fun stayed on the slopes and didn't trickle down to Aspen's famous bar and club scene. The Kennedy kids were wild, always partying, sometimes while skiing. Just last year, RFK's grandson Conor got in a fight at a nightclub in Aspen and was arrested.

I was on the mountain in 1997 when Michael Kennedy died. Halfway down my final run of the day, I noticed that a lot of people were gathered around a tree. It looked like a skier had fallen and broken an arm or leg. Most accidents happen at the end of the day when people are tired. Back at the hotel later, I put on the TV and learned that Michael and a bunch of his friends and relatives were playing ski football—tossing a ball back and forth while skiing downhill at high speeds—when he crashed into the tree, hit his head, and died soon after.

People do stupid things. They take reckless chances.

Not me, and not my kids. I taught them to take their own safety—and the safety of the other people on the slope—very seriously. They don't always listen to me. Ivanka once went skydiving. If I'd known about it beforehand, I would have talked her out of it. "Why would you jump out of a perfectly safe plane?" I asked afterward.

Accidents do happen, though, no matter how much you try to avoid them. When Ivanka was a teenager (this was several years post-divorce), she and I were skiing together in Aspen at Christmastime before she went to her father's place in Palm Beach for New Year's. I took the lead by the tree line and could hear her edges on the ice right behind me. After a few minutes, I realized I couldn't hear her. *She fell?* I wondered. Ivanka is an excellent skier and rarely falls. I went to the ski lift and waited for five minutes . . . and another five. After twenty minutes, I waved down a ski instructor friend of mine and asked, "Have you seen Ivanka?"

He said, "I did. She'll be down soon."

And then I spotted her, skiing toward me slowly. When she was close enough, I saw her eye had a big red blotch around it, and there was blood on her cheek.

"What happened?" I asked.

"A snowboarder ran into me."

She told me that the snowboarder wasn't paying attention at all, and just bombed out from the woods and leveled my daughter. He didn't even stop to see if she was okay.

"Son of a bitch!"

I started looking around for random snowboarders to kill, asking, "Was it him? Or him?" Ivanka couldn't identify the culprit. It happened so fast, she didn't see what he was wearing (probably some dumpy outfit with pants falling down his butt).

"Forget about that, Mom. But what do I tell Dad? He'll never let me ski again."

Oh God. She was right. If he thought Ivanka was in any danger, he'd freak out. I said, "Tell him that you slipped on ice in front of the Little Nell." The Little Nell is the hotel we stayed in.

She did, and he believed her. I'm shocked he didn't sue!

Skiing wasn't the kids' only sport. The boys played soccer. Ivanka had a brief fling with field hockey, an inelegant sport I talked her out of playing, and was on the gymnastics team. They all took karate lessons, which I encouraged for fitness and self-defense. Donald's company renovated Central Park's Wollman Rink, a five-minute walk from Trump Tower, and we took the kids skating on winter weekends. In the summer, they Rollerbladed around Central Park.

Tennis became a big family sport when, in 1985, Donald and

I bought Mar-a-Lago, the 126-room, 110,000-square-foot gilded palace by the sea in Palm Beach, a historic landmark previously owned and built by heiress Marjorie Merriweather Post. We lived right next door to the Bath & Tennis Club. The kids took lessons and became very good players. Donald is pretty good, too. They all played in the club tournaments and were savagely competitive, especially when playing against each other.

Donald put golf clubs in the kids' hands as soon as they were tall enough to swing them. The boys are, to this day, addicted to golf. For the Trump Organization, Eric oversees and opens golf courses all over the world.

I never liked golf. Back when we were dating, Donald tried to get me into it. We went to a golf course that later became the Trump National Doral resort in Miami. I preferred going to the spa rather than the links, but Donald didn't have anyone else to play with that day, so I tagged along. He hit a ball, it landed in the cup, and he started jumping up and down and screaming, "Did you see that! Hole in one!"

I shrugged. "What's the big deal? Isn't it supposed to do that?" I had no clue. I thought people got holes in one all the time.

Donald insisted that I learn the game, or at least give it a good try. He'd learned to ski for me, and even though golf seemed to be about standing around and riding in little carts—not much of an active sport and boring as hell—I agreed.

I hated it right off the bat (or should I say "club"?). The course had a ridiculous rule against women and men playing together, so I had to go out with a bunch of women in patterned skirts and visors who prattled on and on about their kids and grandkids. I hate small chat. Small talk, whatever you call it.

I teed off and hit the ball out of the fairway into the rough. I had to go over there and hunt in the grass to find it. *At least I can get away from these annoying women for a few minutes*, I thought. I found my ball and took a swing at it.

Then I heard a voice even worse than those of the chatty women, a man yelling at me from the other side of the fairway. "Hey! Stop that! What are you doing!" he screeched.

I thought golf was supposed to be a quiet sport.

The burly man in pink pants stormed up to me and said, "You bitch! You took my ball!"

Did I? I didn't realize. I just saw a ball and whacked at it.

"I've got ten thousand dollars on this game! I'm going to kill you!" He shook his club at me.

I walked straight off the course and back to the clubhouse. That was it. I never played golf again. It's too freaking dangerous!

Is fishing a competitive sport? It is for us. My father competed every year in Zlín in a carp fishing contest at the local lake. The winner with the biggest fish would get a prize. He would wake me up before dawn and we'd go to his favorite carp spot. He'd fish all morning and would take his biggest catch to be weighed by the deadline of two p.m. When I was seven, Dedo hadn't caught anything all morning. Then, at one forty-five p.m., he felt a tug on the line, and he reeled in a monster! It wouldn't matter how big it was, though, if we couldn't get the fish to the judges by the deadline. He put this enormous fish in my arms—it was probably half my body weight—and said, "Run, Iva! Run!" I sprinted half a mile to the judges' table with this slippery fish, screaming, "Wait! Wait!" the entire time. At one minute till two, I dropped the fish on the judges' table. Another few seconds, and we wouldn't have won. But we did, and my father and I shared and savored our victory, and the prize of a new fishing rod!

My father taught the boys to fish, too, and they would do it every chance they could. In Greenwich, the boys and my father would set up a little tent in front of Long Island Sound, which bordered the property, and the three of them would sit in there—summer, winter, didn't matter—for hours. Whoever got the biggest catch was the winner of the day, and bragging rights were very important for Trumps. Mar-a-Lago is right on the Intracoastal Waterway, a three-thousand-mile waterway from Boston and around the tip of Florida, popular with migrating fish. My father and the boys would cast their lines from the beach and pull in tunas and big sharks, then let them go. This past March, Don took his sons to Mar-a-Lago for spring break and they caught and released a six-foot-long blacktip shark, and saw eight-hundred-pound hammerheads from shore. For Eric's bachelor party, Don took him to Alaska to fish for salmon, a brothers' bonding trip they try to make every year.

The boys also go hunting often, which I'm not fond of. Don started hunting in boarding school in rural Pennsylvania, and it became a lifelong passion of his—and, by extension, Eric's. I don't object to their going to Patagonia to shoot birds. There are a million of them there, enough to spare. Hunting rabbits in Westchester? No big deal. But why go to Zimbabwe to shoot Bambi and Dumbo? I don't blame people for giving them a hard time about it. I've told them I disagree with shooting animals, but they're grown men. They aren't breaking any laws. As Don recently explained to the *New York Times*, he enjoys the camaraderie with his brother and their friends on a big-game adventure even more than the thrill of the hunt. Sitting in a duck blind for hours not talking is his form of meditation. To each his own. I'd rather sit on a lounge chair at the pool or in the garden.

Sports weren't only for developing a competitive edge. We bonded over our love of activity and being outdoors. One of our most memorable vacations was on horseback. Ivanka was the best rider in our family. She took English-style riding lessons in Greenwich. (Recently, I auctioned off her helmet and made a few thousand dollars for charity.) We all saddled up for a three-day September camping trip in Aspen when the kids were eleven, eight, and five, organized by a friend of mine who owned a horse ranch. My parents were with us in Aspen that year (as they were most years). My mother elected to stay at Little Nell, the hotel, but my father came along with me, Dorothy, the kids, and the cowboy guides on the trail though the mountains and into the valley.

My horse was named Pepsi, and Ivanka's was Cola, both lovely, sweet animals. My father's horse was stung by a bee, took off like a shot, and almost killed him. He survived and we rode on through the trees, which were just turning red, orange, and yellow. We got to the first campground and put out one huge tent for all the girls, and three smaller ones for the guys. The cowboys made our dinner at a campfire. One broke out a guitar and we sang John Denver songs. He gave the guitar to my father, and he played and sang some Czech folk songs. I remember glancing around the campfire as the light danced on my children's faces and thinking how beautiful they were and it all was, the woods and the singing.

And then it started to rain, heavy drops that were so fat, they put out the campfire. We ran for our tents. Ivanka, Dorothy, and I were in the large one. In the rush to get out of the rain, I forgot to watch out for the strings holding the tent in place, tripped over one, and landed face-first in the mud. It was cold away from the fire, so we got into our sleeping bags. I wasn't so happy about that, being wet and covered in mud.

After a few moments of silence, Ivanka asked, "Is it raining *inside* the tent?"

Through a few holes, the rain was leaking in, and the tarp "floor" was turning into a puddle. We didn't have tape to close the hole. I thought, *What can I use to plug it up and stop all that water from getting in? It has to be narrow, absorbent . . .*

"Give me my bag," I said to Dorothy.

I opened it up and found exactly what I needed. "Aha!" I said, holding up a Tampax. I shoved it in the hole and the leaking stopped. I felt like MacGyver, the hero of Don's favorite TV show. Ivanka and Dorothy gave me a round of applause.

An hour later, the tampon landed with a soggy splat on the floor of the tent. I went through my whole box that night. If I needed protection later on the trip, I would have to MacGyver that somehow, too. (Moss?)

The second night, we didn't put the tents up. We slept on cots under the stars in a circle around the campfire. The cowboys formed a second circle outside ours because they heard coyotes nearby. In the middle of the night, I woke to a loud noise. The cowboys were walking around the circle, banging the cooking pots with sticks. I asked the lead cowboy, "Coyotes?"

He said, "Bears."

The kids were thrilled, jumping on the cots, so excited by the idea of seeing an actual bear or a coyote, anything hairy with teeth. I might've dozed for an hour before dawn and woke up feeling and looking like hell. I brushed my teeth in a freezing-cold river with fish in it. I rummaged in my makeup bag for my foundation with sunblock . . . and it was frozen solid.

"That's it," I said. "I'm going back to the hotel to get a massage."

On the third day, the plan was to ride along some trails to a good fishing spot in the valley and make a camp there for our last night, but the horses didn't want to go. They were acting nervous and kept walking in the wrong direction, back toward their home. The cowboys tried to force it, but I said it was okay. The horses had the right idea. When we got back to the ranch, we found out that the team had stepped on porcupine needles. The little spikes were stuck to the bottom of their hooves.

For me, that trip was a near disaster, but the kids talked about it for years. "Remember that time we went camping and it rained all night, and we were almost attacked by bears? Best. Trip. Ever!" What's fun and memorable on a family vacation is always what goes wrong.

We stayed very friendly with the man who ran the ranch, and he amazed us all by deciding to start a line of dog food and pet accessories. His line was a huge success, and now he's worth millions. We were invited to dinner at his cabin in the woods every year. Once, the kids were out sledding and he asked me to put a pizza in the oven for them. By the time they finished, it would be done. But I didn't know how to work his oven and I put the temperature too high. The pizza caught fire and almost burned his cabin to the ground! And he *still* invites us back, every year.

REAL ENRICHMENT

Along with athletes, artists were national heroes in communist Czechoslovakia. Many of my friends in college were musicians, dancers, and painters. Jiří, my first love, was a songwriter. I grew up with a deep appreciation and respect for artists, and the belief that music, fine arts, and dance are the gold of life. Culture feeds the soul. The more time and money you spend on appreciating and making art, the richer you become.

Of course, not all of us are gifted artists. When I was seven, my father's friend, a piano teacher, said to him, "Bring Iva for lessons. Let's see what she's got." My father signed me up. I tried to concentrate, but my heart wasn't in it. I cared a lot more about the chewing gum that my Canadian aunt and uncle sent to me as a gift. You couldn't buy gum in Czechoslovakia, so it was a big deal when a package arrived. I showed off by blowing huge bubbles at piano class, and all the other kids were transfixed (and so jealous!). The teacher called my father and said, "Milos, can you please take Ivana out of my class? She's distracting everyone!" My father sat me down and asked what was going on. I told him the truth: "I love gum and hate piano!" That was that. No more lessons. What would have been the point? My father knew that if I hated it, I would never be good at it. And if you can't be the best, why bother? I don't have regrets about quitting piano so soon. My father tried again and taught me how to play guitar. I was quite good at it as a child, but when I got older, I grew out my nails and that was it for my musical career. I do feel like everyone should know how to play at least one instrument.

Looming large in my living room is a white grand piano that I never play myself. When I have parties, a professional comes to entertain my guests. Nothing is quite as charming as when someone spontaneously slides onto the piano bench or casually picks up a guitar or violin and makes beautiful music for her guests. It's especially charming if a child does it.

When the children were young, they all had at least one year of piano. Ivanka lasted the longest, from seven to nine. I don't think she really liked it. I can't say I liked it, either, when she played the same song eighteen times in a row with mistakes and I had to plaster a supportive smile on my face. After two years, she said, "Do I have to play piano if I don't like it?" It was another echo from my own childhood. Like my father, I didn't force it. I gave her and her brothers every chance to find what they loved and were good at. If they came back from a class and said, "I didn't like it," we'd look around for something else to try. If you excel, it gives you confidence. The arts were another opportunity, like sports and school, to set goals and achieve them.

When Ivanka was eight, she had dreams of being a ballerina. She took classes at Lincoln Center's School of American Ballet and was taught the basics by Russian masters Antonina Tumkovsky and Helene Dudin. She was good enough to be picked to perform in the Christmas production of *The Nutcracker* for two years in a row, dancing the parts of "party scene girl" and "angel." We went as a family to her performances, and it filled my heart with joy and pride to see her dance on the same stage that George Balanchine performed on.

Ivanka gave up her Aspen vacations to stay in New York with Bridget for the two weeks of daily performances. She has credited ballet with teaching her discipline and focus—skills that she uses in every aspect of life—and for giving her a lifelong appreciation for dance that she now shares with her daughter, Arabella, who is as big a dance fan as her mother. Ivanka encourages her daughter by signing her up for lessons and taking her to professional perfor-mances in the American Ballet Theatre in New York and, once, the Mariinsky Theatre in Saint Petersburg, Russia.

Ultimately, Ivanka's ballerina dreams were not to be. She had to give it up when she was ten, even though she still loved it, because she was a head taller than the other girls and double the size of the boys. Oh, well. On to the next.

Fine art has always been very important to me as a collector and a fan. As a charity fund-raiser since the eighties, I've sponsored countless museum events in New York and beyond. Recently, I hosted an exhibit called "Born Wild" in Miami for French artist Richard Orlinski, most famous for his monumental mountain-top sculptures of bears, gorillas, and wolves at the French Alps ski resort Courchevel. We raised $80,000 for the people of Haiti, and Richard was so grateful, he gave me the signature piece from the exhibit, a three-meter-high rearing stallion in red that stands on the coffee table in my Miami living room. It makes me smile whenever I look at it.

Every home I've had, I've filled with beautiful objects—and that includes the creations of my children. Ivanka took drawing and painting classes at the Museum of Modern Art in the early nineties. At that time, the whole city was buzzing about an eight-day-only installation of works by Matisse and Picasso, including the masterpiece *Les Demoiselles d'Avignon*. I had a party, and as always, the kids were there to greet my guests and make small talk with them. One guest mentioned the installation, and Ivanka, around twelve, started talking about it, having seen and studied the paintings as part of her lessons at the museum that week. I just stood there and watched my adult friends ask my sixth-grade daughter for her insight about Picasso, thinking, *That's my girl!*

Even if she'd never picked up a pencil or paintbrush again, the classes were worth it to put her inside a museum every week. Being exposed to and educated about art when you're young gives you a lifelong appreciation for it. Our tastes differ, but Ivanka and I share the love of immersing ourselves in our aesthetic. My style is luxurious, whimsical. In my town house on East Sixty-Fourth Street, I have a leopard room with spotted wallpaper and upholstery, and feline-themed art. My red and green living room is how Louis XVI would have lived if he had had money. Ivanka and Jared Kushner, her husband, like modern, minimalist style. They're art fans and have collected pieces by Louis Eisner, Alex Israel, Garry Winogrand, and Christopher Wool, among others. Her new house in Kalorama, Washington, DC, is sparsely decorated in muted grays and whites. It's the opposite of how I decorate, but as long as she's happy, her style is okay by me.

Don was just not into the arts. He knew this about himself very early, and there was no point in pushing him to do things he couldn't have cared less about. But Eric was very creative, the kind of kid who was always busy with art projects. He took drawing classes at MoMA, too, and was into painting watercolors for a while. I framed them and hung them in Greenwich and my post-divorce Palm Beach house Concha Marina. My second husband (technically my third, but Austrian Fred doesn't count), Riccardo Mazzucchelli, a patron of the arts, a serious collector of Eastern European masters' paintings, and a talented craftsman, was a great influence on Eric. Riccardo set up a pottery studio in Greenwich with a few wheels and a kiln. I remember many weekends in the studio with the two of them, molding clay on a huge table into bowls and little statues. I made a leopard that is currently displayed in the leopard room (where else?). Eric made hundreds of ceramic objets d'art, painting them carefully with glaze. Riccardo would get up in the middle of the night to turn off the kiln to make sure Eric's pieces didn't explode. I had a thousand original Eric ashtrays all over the house for years, despite the fact that no one smoked.

ERIC

When I went to boarding school, I fell in love with woodworking. They had a shop program there with a great teacher named Mr. Block (an ironic name, given his profession). I built a twenty-two-foot-long rowing scull and designed all sorts of Shaker-style furniture: benches, tables, everything that you could imagine. Any free time at boarding school when I wasn't in class, playing sports, or studying, I was in the shop building.

I HATE PLAYDATES

Above sports and the arts, Donald and I placed the highest value on the kids' education. I was in charge of choosing all of their schools. Getting accepted into a private nursery school in Manhattan in the eighties wasn't as much of a blood sport as it is today, but it was competitive. I don't really know what the admissions officers were looking for in a three-year-old, but the politeness and manners training I'd been working on with the kids—always saying "please" and "thank you," smiling, and looking adults in the eye when they're speaking to you—didn't hurt. They went to Christ Church Day School on Park Avenue and East Sixtieth Street. It was only a few blocks from Trump Tower and two blocks from Central Park. It couldn't have been a more convenient location for me or the nanny to run them over in the morning, pick them up in the afternoon, go to the park for playtime, and then go home for dinner.

Preschool admission was just a warm-up for the much longer, more complicated process at grade school that included tours, testing, and evaluations. Why does a kindergartner need recommendations? They weren't trying to get into medical school! As strange as it was, I took the process seriously because I knew how important it was for the kids to get the best possible education from day one.

Some of the schools we looked at were for supersmart kids who, at six, were computer and math geniuses; these schools had very tough curriculums. Some schools were for the little dummies of rich parents, basically drawing and sandbox time for $20,000 a year. I was looking for a balance: schools with top-notch sports, arts, and academics in a smart, friendly environment.

For Don, a competitive, sports-obsessed kid, I choose Buckley, an all-boys school on East Seventy-Third between Park and Lexington.

Ivanka went to Chapin, a small all-girls school with a cozy, nurturing vibe (Jackie Kennedy was an alum) on East End Avenue and East Eighty-Fourth Street.

For Eric, I went with a coed experience at Trinity on West Ninety-First between Amsterdam and Columbus.

Three kids at three different schools in three different Manhattan neighborhoods. The logistics of just getting them there was a nightmare. We had limos and company cars with drivers to take them. Don and Eric sometimes took a bus that pulled up right in front of Trump Tower.

Chapin admissions required a series of interviews with school personnel, first with Donald and me, then Ivanka, then all three of us together. It was endless. I always dressed well, usually in a business suit, because I was coming from work at the Plaza Hotel and returning there afterward. When Ivanka went to her interviews, she wore dresses and tights, Mary Janes, and her hair pulled back from her face. The other mothers on the tours weren't professionally dressed, and their kids were usually in jeans and T shirts. I wondered if Ivanka and I might have overdressed, but then the other mothers started asking me for interview style advice for themselves and their daughters. I didn't know any better than they did! We must have been doing it right, because Ivanka was accepted and took her place in a class of only fifty girls. She loved going there.

I kept a close eye on the children's academic progress during homework hour and by scrutinizing their quarterly grades. If they dipped below a B+ in any subject, we sat down and talked about what the problem was and worked to get their scores up. Their schools were top-echelon, very competitive, and full of the children of the superrich. Parents spared no expense to put their kids at the head of the class. It was common for them to spend big bucks on tutors for their seven-year-olds.

Not me. I was already paying plenty to send them to these schools and expected the teachers to do the teaching, not private tutors. If the kids needed help, they got it from me. History wasn't my strong suit. They'd ask me about things that happened hundreds of years ago and I would say, "I live in the now! I'm more interested in tomorrow than yesterday!" Math was my forte. Before going out for the night, I'd sit at the table in a designer couture gown with fifty pounds of beading, full makeup, and hair up to the ceiling, with algebra books open in front of us, scratching out formulas with sharpened number-two pencils. When they erased a mistake and left little rubber clumps on the paper, I'd yell, "Brush away from the dress!" God forbid some of those pink eraser crumbs got stuck in the beading.

Ivanka was very popular at Chapin, always invited to every party and in high demand for playdates. She was, and is, sweet, friendly, and pretty. I can't imagine why anyone *wouldn't* want to be her friend. That said, I got the feeling that some of the girls pursued her because her parents' photos appeared in the newspapers with celebrities at fashion shows, concerts, and parties, and in our box seats at Yankee Stadium and the US Open tennis tournament.

Donald used to tell the kids "Don't trust anyone" as an early business lesson, but it also applied to friendships. I grew up wary of everyone outside our family and closest friends, always conscious of the possibility that a chatty neighbor could be a communist spy. I didn't take loyalty and trust lightly then, and I don't now. I have to be careful about confiding in people, because everything I say— and a lot of things I *never* said—could turn up in the papers or online. Former friends and employees have lied to the press about me. One of my boyfriends (after husband number three) tried to blackmail me for money. I thought he was a nice man, and then he stupidly threatened me with Photoshopped pictures. I called the FBI, and two days later, he left the country and my lawyer Gary Lyman coordinated with the FBI to make sure he never entered the US again. You'd think people would know not to mess with me (or my lawyer).

My wariness might've passed down to the kids. I never discouraged them from having playdates, disapproved of their friendships, or said, "You are not allowed to see _____." If they could make time in their busy schedules between sports, lessons, homework, and family outings, they could have as many as playdates as they liked . . . at their friends' houses. I did discourage playdates at Trump Tower. The triplex was just too huge and lavish. "You live *here?*" the friends would say, and you could see the intimidation, awe, jealousy, or resentment on their little faces. In an instant, my children would be judged on their parents' wealth and not their own character, for good or bad. Their classmates would then talk to each other, and the children would be singled out as "different." Even among this population—the offspring of Manhattan's elite— none had their names in gigantic gold letters on the side of their own building. The inevitable result would be negative.

The only person who had an open invitation to come to the triplex for playdates whenever he wanted was Michael Jackson.

The King of Pop lived in Trump Tower and was a good friend of our whole family. He'd stop by and chat with Donald and me for twenty minutes, and then he'd go up to the kids' floor to hang out with them for hours and hours. They'd watch MTV, play Mario Brothers or Tetris, and build Trump Tower in Legos. Michael was a thirty-year-old kid. He could relate to Ivanka and the boys better than to us.

When Ivanka performed in *The Nutcracker*, Michael, at the peak of his fame, went to a performance and caused a near riot in the audience, as well as some backstage controversy. One of the teenage ballerinas heard he was coming and got the idea that they should all wear one white glove, an homage to his signature style. The teachers were horrified, and the teen dancer was taken to task for even thinking of compromising the costumes of the production. Ivanka was mortified to be the indirect cause of the tension, but she didn't let it affect her performance. Michael told me that she looked like an angel that night.

For the record, during those playdates with Michael, the nannies or I was always in the room. My read on him was asexual. He was a child himself in a man's body, tender, sweet, and gentle. I never believed the accusations that he molested those kids. There's no way he could have hurt anyone.

In Greenwich, the kids had their weekend friends, the children of our neighbors. I remember Ivanka hosting sleepover parties there—I would have to yell to get her and her five girlfriends to go to sleep before three a.m. Eric and Don would ride bikes and roam the woods with a pack of boys for hours. They had a set of friends in Palm Beach, too. But no matter where we were, my three kids were each other's best friends and constant companions.

I've heard that being a parent to a school-age child zooms you back to your own schooltime issues and insecurities. Would I be popular with the other mothers? Would they include me in coffee dates and aerobics classes? Would they invite me on *playdates*?

I could not have cared less.

I avoided playdates like the plague. The nannies did all the dropping-off and picking-up duties. I was working nonstop at the hotels and was just too busy to bond with the other moms. It was a challenge to show up for all three kids' Parents' Days, recitals, concerts, games, plays, and graduation ceremonies. I admit, I missed a few. My rule was that *someone*—me, Donald, the nannies, my parents, or a combination—had to be at every one. I had a strategy for going to the events with the best possible time efficiency. I'd take a car to the school, sit in a seat that my mother or Dorothy saved for me, watch the performance, and cheer on my child. I'd find them afterward for a kiss, hug, and congratulations, and then I'd be out the door and back at my desk within an hour. Later that night at dinner, we'd discuss the performance in detail. Parent-teacher conferences had a high priority. Donald always came to those, and usually let me do the talking. I'd book it into my schedule well in advance, to make enough time for an in-depth conversation. I'd prepare a list of questions beforehand, and if I didn't like the answers, I'd work with the teachers and administrators to make the necessary adjustments.

The energy and effort I put into the kids' schools were about academics and extracurriculars only. I didn't have the bandwidth for volunteering. The majority of moms who tried to rope me into committees were stay-at-home moms with no work obligations. Those committees, I heard, were really about socializing, gossiping, and complaining anyway. If I had a complaint, I went directly to the dean, and I saw no point in gossiping with the moms. The women were good people and highly involved in their children's lives, but I just had nothing to say to them and no time to say it. I barely made it to baby showers for some of my nearest and dearest.

I'm just not the kind of woman who casts a net for new friends. My core group and I have known each other for forty years. Dorothy can tell you exactly who is my best friend, just a friend, a social climber, a user, an abuser, or a nobody. She's the gatekeeper of my life and knows who to put right through and who to get rid of. Again, it's about loyalty and trust. How many best friends do you really have? Four? Five? That's it. You don't need more than that if the bonds are deep.

Casual friendships actually cause problems for me. To this day, people I meet once or twice will use the wafer-thin connection to call restaurants and make reservations under my name. Recently, I got a call from the Polo Bar on East Fifty-Fifth Street, a popular restaurant in the city. Some nights, you couldn't get a reservation even if your life depended on it. The maître d' said, "Hello, Ivana. Did you make a reservation for fourteen people for Saturday night?"

I said, "No! I'm in Miami!"

The reservation problem is a little-known hazard of being famous. A dozen maître d's in New York, Miami, and Saint-Tropez have me on speed dial to confirm bookings in my name. "If I made the reservation, I'll be there," I tell them. "If I'm not, call the cops!"

HAPPY BIRTHDAY!

When Ivanka was at Chapin, one of the girls in her class had a Las Vegas birthday party. Not a Las Vegas–*themed* party, which would have been strange enough. The plan was to fly the birthday girl—I think she was fourteen—and all her friends to Nevada for an overnight in a casino hotel suite, spend a day on the strip, and then fly back the next day.

I thought about calling the hosts and reminding them that Atlantic City had hundreds of luxurious suites, including Trump Castle's, and was only a few hours away by car. No need to fly a dozen New York kids across the country to see the bright lights. For that matter, you could take them to the Grand Hyatt or the Plaza, order room service, and go to see *Cats* or *Les Miz* for a fraction of the cost.

For the life of me, I could not understand the point of this trip. They thought Sin City was an appropriate destination for a bunch of teenage girls? It's possible there was a concert or event that had special meaning to the birthday girl, but still. The only reason this party stuck with me among all the kids' friends' parties over the years was the sheer stupidity of it.

Ivanka wanted to go, of course. The party seemed ridiculous to me, but it sounded like a lot of fun to her. I said, "If you're caught up on your schoolwork, you can go." Unfortunately, she had an exam scheduled for the day they were flying back. That made the decision easy. Unless she could reschedule the exam, she couldn't go on the trip. Her teacher refused. Donald called the school and asked politely if the exam could be postponed by one day. The teacher wouldn't budge. It might have been the only time Donald was told no.

When I tell this story, people often ask, "Did she cry and beg you to let her go?"

Not one tear. Not one whine. My children never talked back. If I said, "You can't go," you couldn't go. That was it. Now, if Ivanka had come back to me with a very good reason to go to this absurd party, I would have heard her out . . . and still said no. My priority was her education, not trashy entertainment. She knew that already, and there was no point in challenging the decision of the boss.

Over-the-top kid-party extravaganzas were a matter of course in New York and Los Angeles in the eighties and nineties, with parents spending tens of thousands on their children's fifth or tenth birthdays, hundreds of thousands on Sweet Sixteens and bar and bat mitzvahs. The gifts were insane: BMWs, Benzes, Dolce & Gabbana shopping sprees, a trip to Paradise Island for fifty.

Babi and me in Zlín, 1949.

A rare dress-up day in Zlín, circa 1958.

Carving up the Alps for the Czech national juniors team, circa 1967.

Modeling in Prague during college in high style, circa 1968.

At Concha Marina in Palm Beach, circa 1995.

Publicity photo for the release of my first novel, *For Love Alone*, in 1992.

Skiing in Aspen in the nineties. No puffy coats or knit hats for me, ever!

Making friends
with the pigeons in
Piazza San Marco,
Venice, Italy, circa
2005.

Just engaged in Aspen,
1976.

The weekend I met
Donald for the first
time in New York,
1976.

Don Jr. and baby Ivanka, 1982.

Eric flashing his baby blues in 1985.

Don Jr., Donald, me, and Fred Trump at Winged Foot Golf Club, Mamaroneck, NY, 1978.

Wedding day, 1977, in Manhattan. From left to right: Fred Trump, Mary Trump, Donald, me, my father, and my aunt.

Eric's sixth birthday party at the Plaza Hotel, New York City, 1990. Within a month, Donald and I split.

Mother-daughter photo shoot, circa 1991.

Our Aspen camping trip in 1989. My horse was named Pepsi; Ivanka's was named Cola. Despite being attacked by bees, bears, and storms, the kids loved it.

Trudy the nanny with Don Jr., 1978.

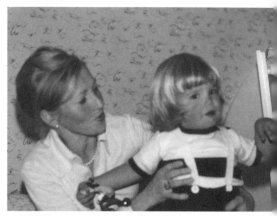

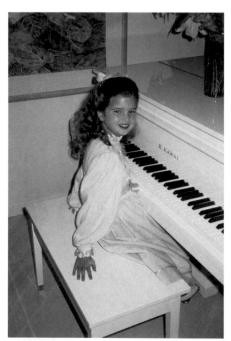

Ivanka took two years of piano lessons, reluctantly, circa 1988.

Don Jr. and Ivanka in his room at Trump Tower, 1992.

From left to right: Don Jr., Babi, Ivanka, Chappy, me, and Eric, 1992.

An eighties headband moment with Don Jr., circa 1986.

Left: Another Plaza birthday party. Ivanka loved those velvet dresses and the boys looked adorable in their little suits, circa 1987. *Right:* Ivanka in her angel costume backstage at the New York City Ballet's Lincoln Center production of *The Nutcracker,* 1990.

On Riccardo's yacht, cruising the Mediterranean, circa 1993.

Left: Christmas in Aspen, here with my father and Don Jr., circa 1987.
Right: Ivanka and Dedo at the pool in Greenwich, circa 1986.

With Roffredo and the Ferrari he gave me in New York, 1999.

Ivanka with Bridget Carroll, circa 1991.

Don Jr. at Atlantis in the Bahamas, circa 2007.

The brothers. A summer moment somewhere off the coast of France, circa 1995.

With my Madame Tussauds wax likeness in New York, 2000.

Teenage Ivanka in her room on East Sixty-Fourth Street, circa 1994, on the phone as always!

It must have been a nautical theme night, with my parents in the late eighties in Palm Beach.

Eel for dinner, *again?* Don Jr. doesn't look too happy about it. Summer in Greece, 1993.

Eric was taller than me by the time he was twelve. Summer on the boat, circa 1996.

An early modeling shoot for Ivanka, 1997.

Don Jr.'s mullet moment in Aspen. You can see the rest of us in his sunglasses, circa 1995.

Thanksgiving in Greenwich, with a gigantic turkey and helpful Ivanka. I'd start cooking at five a.m. to feed a small army of Trumps, 1988.

At Eric and Lara's wedding with the entire family at Mar-a-Lago, 2014.

In front of my Manhattan town house, circa 2008. On the left, Dorothy Curry, the kids' former nanny and my right-hand woman.

Tiger (and my legs) in Miami, 2015.

Wedding day, 1995, in Manhattan. Left to right: Babi, Riccardo, me, and Ivanka, wearing the gold mermaid dress we traded back and forth for years to come.

With Rossano, circa 2007.

M.Y. Ivana, cruising the French Riviera, circa 2005.

Decisions, decisions. (I chose the handsome Italian on my left.) With Henrik and Roffredo on my yacht, 1998.

Graduation day for Ivanka from Wharton, 2004.

With my first grandchild, Kai, and her daddy in 2007. Eight more would arrive over the next ten years.

With two of my other babies, Chappy 2 and Dodo, circa 2001.

We Trumps weren't exactly modest and unassuming. During my marriage to Donald and after, I have been known to enjoy the good life, and that includes parties and galas, and openings of clubs and restaurants. I have hosted fabulous celebrations all over the world for myself, friends, and charities, some of them attended by Don, Eric, and Ivanka. My philosophy for throwing parties is to go big, have fun, and do it right. I'm a genius with setting a beautiful table, seating charts, and menus. BUT—I did *not* throw pull-out-all-the-stops blowouts for my children or shower them with mountains of luxurious gifts. Their parties were always within a sensible and appropriate range. If a five-, ten-, or fifteen-year-old sees that his parents break the bank just because it's his birthday, he will believe he is God's gift to humanity. He'll assume his parents will do *anything* he wants. It's the key ingredient in the recipe for raising a spoiled brat. A one-year-old child doesn't remember a party anyway, so the birthday celebrations for my kids until age six or so were small gatherings in the apartment for pizza, cake, and ice cream with friends and family.

Later on, after we bought the Plaza Hotel in 1987, the catering and banquet services would set up a dozen tables in meeting rooms and decorate them with balloons and confetti, colorful table settings, and centerpieces for kid parties. We always invited the parents, too, and served them hors d'oeuvres or drinks from the open bar. It was the only day every year I put time into talking to them, but, as the host, I could make a quick escape if the conversation was horrible. I preferred to concentrate on the kids and make sure they were getting all the burgers, cupcakes, and soda they wanted anyway.

With twenty kids, all their parents, and our friends and

family—we hated to leave anyone out—there might be a hundred people in the room. The cakes, made by the Plaza's pastry chef, were enormous—often with a few tiers.

Since we used the same setting every year, we mixed things up with specialized entertainment like clowns and magicians. Ivanka's birthday is October 30, so it was only natural to have a Halloween theme with all the kids—and their parents—in costume. Ivanka veered toward pretty princess costumes, anything with leotards, tights, and ballet slippers. One year, she dressed as a ballerina, Eric was a toy soldier in a red coat with gold buttons, and Don was GI Joe in head-to-toe camo. Looking at this photo now, I see how clearly the costumes reflect their roles in the family. Eric, the youngest, was like a toy for Ivanka and Don. They played with him and molded him. When they were older, Ivanka gave him style tips on how to dress his best. Don was both of their protectors, a soldier who had his little sister's and brother's backs. Ivanka was the outgoing performer who wanted attention and bloomed in the spotlight.

Don's birthday was New Year's Eve, so his parties were always in Aspen. We invited our in-town friends to our hotel suite for dinner and cake, and to sing "Happy Birthday" to him. Then Donald and I would go to a restaurant or club with our friends, and the kids would stay in the hotel with my parents. They were allowed to watch the ball drop in Times Square on TV and would tell their friends that they got to stay up until midnight, but it was really only ten p.m. in Colorado. Until Don turned ten, he thought the celebrations and fireworks on his birthday were for him! When we came back to the city, we'd close Wollman Rink to the public and invite Don's class and their parents for a skating party with hot chocolate and cake.

Eric's birthday, on January 6, came one week after Don's, so sometimes we celebrated with one big party for both. Once, we sectioned off an area in front of the Plaza for a show with circus dogs. During the boys' karate phase, we hired a sensei to do a demonstration. He broke piles of wood with his hands and split a brick with his forehead. He showed the kids how to fend off an attacker and, with a swift move, threw his assistant onto his back on the mat. Then he said, "Who'd like to learn how to do that? Any volunteers?"

Not a peep from dozens of boys.

Then Ivanka raised her hand and said, "I'll do it!"

As for gifts, sorry to disappoint you if you think we bought them diamond-encrusted tennis rackets, mini Land Rovers, or Shetland ponies with satin bows around their necks. The biggest presents we gave were new bikes or skis, or a couple of party dresses for Ivanka. Her birthday was right before the holidays, and the boys' were right after. If we piled on the gifts, it would have been overkill. They felt the same way, telling me outright it was embarrassing to open excessive gifts in front of their friends.

I would beg my friends not to give them gifts. I can't stand it when people send me things that I don't need or want, which is everything! Then you have to reciprocate and lose half a day shopping. It's a pain in the neck. You both get sucked into a tradition of sending each other gifts. Stop! Please do not send me anything. If you absolutely must, keep it small, like a nice scented candle or an orchid. Huge gift baskets with candies and cookies? I give them right to Dorothy. (She would like to interject to say that you can continue to send those and other small gifts.)

Of course, people ignored my request and the gift mountain was absurdly high. We made a family tradition of going through all the toys, sports equipment, clothes, and games, and sorting them into piles. One pile was for the keepers, things they loved and were genuinely excited to have. Doubles (or triples) of that year's hot toy, or things they already had or didn't *really* want, went into the donation pile. We sent them to local charities like the Salvation Army, the Red Cross, and Lighthouse for the Blind. The tradition of giving stuck with all of my kids. Eric has made me so proud by raising over $10 million for St. Jude Children's Research Hospital via his charitable foundation and annual golf club dinner and auction. Don raises money for Operation Smile. Ivanka fund-raises for Habitat for Humanity and the Children's Aid Society, among others.

The other, less gratifying post-party tradition in our house: writing thank-you notes. Every single person who came to the party got one. If Mrs. Schlemiel gave a Walkman, she would get a note. If Mr. Schlimazel gave a teddy bear, he would get a note. My kids would have to write *hundreds* of them after each birthday. It was a huge operation, taking over the dining room table with stationery, envelopes, lists of names and addresses, and stamps. Handwritten thanks (as opposed to using computers) gave the notes a meaningful personal touch. I raised my kids to put manners and politeness first. If someone took the time to shop for a gift, the least my kids could do was take the time to write a proper note.

As they got older, we stopped having big parties. They were at school or wanted to celebrate with their friends. I'd take them to a nice lunch in Aspen or invite them for a weekend at Concha Marina. My gifts didn't change, though. For Ivanka, I still give her beautiful dresses or handbags. The boys always want new skis or fishing rods or, nowadays, electronics.

I've noticed a generational shift in how Don and Ivanka handle their own children's birthday parties. They're usually at a play space in Manhattan where the kids can run around and go crazy in a ball pit or on a trampoline. They're very casual, and limited to family and a dozen or so guests. No tiered wedding cakes, just simple sheet cakes or something homemade with candles. My kids are less formal with their children than I was with mine. It's a generational thing. In the end, it doesn't matter where you throw the party or how big it is, as long as the child feels special and loved.

HAPPY HOLIDAYS!

How did the Trumps celebrate the holidays? Just like other American families . . . with a few extra bells and whistles.

HALLOWEEN

When we lived at 800 Fifth Avenue (before Eric was born), trick-or-treating was easy. The kids dressed up and took their little plastic pumpkins door-to-door in the building with the nannies and me smiling behind them. After we moved to Trump Tower, going door-to-door wasn't appropriate. A lot of the apartment owners traveled and weren't around, or they didn't like kids knocking on their doors. Instead, we'd take the kids to Fifth Avenue and Park Avenue and buzzed their friends' apartments, or we'd go to a party hosted by a classmate. If Halloween fell on a weekend, we'd be in Greenwich. The suburbs were better for trick-or-treating—fewer cars and more of a kid-friendly environment—and the children would run from house to house for candy. I got a lot of exercise keeping up. By the mideighties, when Donald and I had become very well-known, I was worried about the kids trick-or-treating with just the nannies, so our security men would follow them, incognito. I don't think they're aware to this day that the security guards were watching them.

THANKSGIVING

This was my holiday to host the extended Trump family—twenty-five people—in Greenwich. With seventeen bedrooms, the house was big enough for a long-weekend sleepover. First, we'd decorate. The entrance was a three-story rotunda, with two staircases climbing up on either side. We got a huge tree, twenty feet tall at least, and positioned it between the staircases. I had hundreds of spectacular crystal-ball ornaments from Czechoslovakia. The kids would hang them on the bottom branches, and the houseman would use a ladder to reach the top. The tree was so huge, it'd take two weeks to decorate. I have been known to leave my trees up through January. Don made me laugh when he sent me a photo of his family's tree this year that was left in the living room for so long, it turned brown. Apparently, holding on to the holiday spirit as long as possible became a strange and funny family tradition.

I got up at five a.m. to cook a traditional American Thanksgiving feast, dressing a twenty-five-pound turkey with liver, raisin, and nut stuffing. Our side dishes were mashed potatoes, grilled vegetables, and my homemade cranberry sauce. For dessert, apple tart with ice cream.

ERIC

My favorite holiday growing up was Thanksgiving. We would all cook. My mom would make traditional cranberry sauce with whole cranberries. But as kids, my brother, sister, and I always liked the cranberry sauce that plopped out of the can that you could slice. It just tasted better. She worked for hours stewing her sauce, and we'd end up eating the Ocean Spray gelatin wafers.

Growing up, we had two November holidays: November 1 is All Saints' Day, a Catholic holiday for acknowledging the saints; November 2 is All Souls' Day (in Czech, it's Dušičky, or "Little Souls"), a holiday for the dead, observed by visiting graves, lighting candles, and laying wreaths. If the dates fell midweek, you would celebrate the following weekend. Growing up, on Dušičky, my mother would cook Segedin goulash with sauerkraut and chicken paprika with cabbage. Although my parents didn't come to Thanksgiving in Greenwich, they lived with us in the US for at least six months of the year throughout the kids' lives. My mother cooked all her classic Czech dishes for the kids and made sure they ate every single bite.

ERIC

Babi was always a rock in our lives, a grounding force. And her cooking! She made strawberry dumplings and chicken

paprika, which we all loved. She has a very different attitude than parents or grandparents today who are focused on eating healthy. She came out of the Soviet bloc. You weren't worrying about using four sticks of butter in a recipe. In fact, if you had four sticks of butter, you were lucky. She would make you eat three servings, and even if you were about to pop, she'd throw more on your plate. I actually found her chicken paprika recipe recently and tried to make it the other day. It was unbelievable. Sauté chicken and add tons of sour cream and butter.

She never wasted food. I remember going to nice restaurants and watching her wrap up rolls that were left on the table and put them in her purse. Her "do not waste a crumb" mentality came from things she saw as a young girl in Czechoslovakia—World War II atrocities and the Russian invasions, people going hungry, parents not being able to feed their children. Babi came over to America and she started experiencing a different life than she had lived overseas, but she never lost her roots.

In the Greenwich house, when I was a little kid, I remember getting in Babi's bed with her and Don and Ivanka; eating hot dogs, strawberry ice cream, and Klondike bars; watching *Wheel of Fortune* on this old gray Zenith TV; and feeling really happy. To this day, she remains an amazing person who's devoted to Donnie, Ivanka, me, our mom, and all her great-grandchildren.

BABI'S FAMOUS CHICKEN PAPRIKA
Serves 8

INGREDIENTS

*1 whole fryer chicken
    (about 2½ pounds)
2½ tablespoons flour
½ teaspoon salt
½ teaspoon white pepper
2½ tablespoons sweet
    Hungarian paprika
1½ tablespoons butter*

*1½ tablespoons vegetable oil
1 cup finely chopped yellow
    onion
2 cups well-seasoned chicken
    stock
1 cup sour cream
Noodles or rice*

INSTRUCTIONS

1. Cut up and disjoint the chicken.

2. Dust the chicken pieces with ½ tablespoon of the flour seasoned with the salt, white pepper, and ½ tablespoon of the paprika.

3. In a heavy saucepan, melt the butter over medium heat. Add the vegetable oil. Sauté the chicken until browned, about 7 minutes, and remove from the pan.

4. In the same pan, sauté the onion with the remaining 2 tablespoons paprika for 3 to 4 minutes. When the onions are translucent, return the chicken to the pan and add the stock. Simmer, covered, until tender, about 1 hour.

5. Slowly stir in the remaining 2 tablespoons flour and the sour cream. Simmer 10 minutes, until thickened and smooth. Do not boil or the sour cream could separate.

6. Serve with noodles or rice.

GOULASH FOR BEGINNERS

Serves 8

INGREDIENTS

2 tablespoons vegetable oil

4 white onions, chopped

4 pounds beef, cubed

1 tablespoon paprika, plus more
    to taste

2 cups water

1 Knorr beef bouillon cube

1 tablespoon Wondra flour

Noodles, potatoes, or dumplings

Salt and pepper

INSTRUCTIONS

1. Heat the oil in a heavy saucepan over medium heat and sauté the onions until pink.

2. Add the beef to the onions and stir together. Add 1 tablespoon paprika and stir. Cook the meat until browned, about 5 minutes.

3. Cover with water and simmer for 25 minutes, adding the rest of the water a little at a time to keep the meat covered.

4. Add the bouillon cube and stir until dissolved. Add more paprika to taste. Add the flour and stir. Simmer until the meat is soft, another 30 minutes. Add water as needed.

5. Serve over noodles, potatoes, or dumplings.

6. Add salt and pepper to taste.

IVANKA'S FAVORITE STRAWBERRY DUMPLINGS
Serves 4

INGREDIENTS

For the dough:
½ cup all-purpose flour
½ cup Wondra flour
1 egg
Salt
Water

For the filling:
1 pint cleaned fresh strawberries
9 ounces farmer cheese, crumbled
6 tablespoons butter, melted
2 cups powdered sugar, sifted
Zest of 1 lemon
Sprig of fresh mint

INSTRUCTIONS

1. Bring a large pot of water to a boil.

2. Combine the flours, egg, salt, and enough water to make a soft dough. Knead until smooth and springy.

3. Wrap a piece of the dough large enough to cover a whole strawberry around each berry.

4. Place the wrapped strawberries in the boiling water for 5 to 7 minutes.

5. While the dumplings cook, make the filling: combine the cheese, butter, powdered sugar, and lemon zest in a bowl.

6. Remove the dumplings from the water and place on a warm serving tray.

7. Cover the dumplings with the cheese mixture.

8. Garnish each with a sprig of mint and serve hot.

ERIC LOVES LEČO

Serves 8

INGREDIENTS

1 medium onion, chopped

1 tablespoon vegetable oil

2 beef Polska kielbasas, sliced
   into discs

8 to 10 green peppers, diced

8 to 10 red tomatoes, diced

1 Knorr beef bouillon cube

8 eggs, beaten

Salt and pepper

2 tablespoons sour cream

INSTRUCTIONS

1. In a heavy saucepan, sauté the onion in the oil for 3 to 4 minutes until translucent.

2. Add the sausage slices, the peppers, and the tomatoes. Crumble in the bouillon cube and cook until soft, about 5 minutes.

3. Add the eggs and stir for about 5 minutes or until the eggs are set.

4. Season with salt and pepper to taste, and top with a dollop of sour cream. Serve immediately.

CHRISTMAS

When I was a girl, Christmas dinners featured traditional Czech delicacies like hard-boiled eggs with caviar, breaded and sautéed carp, German potato salad, and a strudel for dessert. The Trump Christmas tradition was all about Aspen. (On the rare occasions we were stuck in Manhattan for Christmas Eve, Donald and I went to midnight Mass at Saint Patrick's Cathedral and then to a reception afterward behind the altar with Cardinal John O'Connor.) We flew to Colorado in a private 727, which was always a nail-biter because the Aspen runway was very short and positioned between two mountains. Most pilots preferred to go to Denver. To make a safe landing in Aspen, the weather had to agree with you, and the pilot had to time it perfectly. Even scarier than landing? Taking off. The pilot would put his foot on the brake, rev the engine, and come off the brake suddenly, and the plane would lift straight up. Even with no snow or wind, I'd hold my breath. The kids had no idea what was going on; they trusted our pilots. Donald didn't like traveling with the whole family on one plane in case something happened and would sometimes put the kids and nannies on a commercial flight. Fred Trump was the same way. I wouldn't call it superstitious, though; more like a philosophy of hoping for the best and planning for the worst.

Our holiday home away from home was the Little Nell, a hotel right on the mountain owned by Marvin Davis, an industrialist, movie company owner, and real estate magnate. We had the same three suites every year. One had three bedrooms for the kids. Another had two bedrooms for my parents and Dorothy or Bridget. The last was for Donald and me. At night, from my bed, I would watch the lights on the snowcats as they groomed the slopes, leaving trails in the powder like corduroy pants. Each suite had its own living room and terrace overlooking the mountain.

Once we'd organized our luggage in the suites and had a snack, we'd head straight out on snowmobiles into the valley to pick out a Christmas tree. We only wanted the top eight feet, so the boys would climb a fifteen-foot tree and saw off that much. It'd flip down to the snow, which was as high as your waist. Then we'd tie the tree to the backs of the snowmobiles and drag it to the hotel. We'd carry it through the lobby and down a long corridor to our master suite, leaving a trail of sappy needles along the way. The hotel staff would take our boxes of ornaments out of hotel storage and put them in the suite when we arrived. Once the tree was in place in the master suite, we'd decorate it. When we left in January, the staff would come in and take down the ornaments, repack and store them, and clean the needles off the carpet and the multitude of strays scattered all over the hotel. They were not too happy with us about that. One year, we arrived in our suites to find a faux Christmas tree already set up in the usual spot and decorated! Attention, Little Nell staffers: message received.

In Czechoslovakia, we give the gifts on Christmas Eve. But Don, Eric, and Ivanka are Americans, so we followed the custom of opening presents on Christmas morning. After the kids went to bed, we'd put the gifts under the tree as if we were Santa, and at dawn, they would be wide-awake, tearing the wrapping off their presents while my parents, Donald, and I sipped coffee and wished we were back in bed. Each kid would receive only a handful of gifts. They'd make a list and I'd pick out three items, plus one or two surprises. That evening, we'd get dressed up—the boys in suits and ties, Ivanka in a velvet dress—and have eggnog (for the adults) and hot chocolate (for the kids) with some friends in our suite before we headed to the hotel restaurant for dinner. I wore a slinky maxi dress with a silk-screened Santa Claus on the front, perhaps the only dress I repeated often in public.

ERIC

Every year, we'd drive for half an hour outside Aspen, then throw on cross-country skis and ski to a charming log cabin called the Pine Creek Cookhouse for dinner. We'd stay there for a couple of hours eating a huge, heavy dinner, then we'd all cross-country ski, totally full, a couple miles back to the car. On the way to the restaurant, it was uphill. The way back was all downhill, which is actually really tough on cross-country skis. You're stuck in two parallel tracks with no way to stop. It was always pitch-black outside, so we wore headlamps to see five feet in front of us. Everyone was wiping out and getting covered in snow. Don was usually in the front of the line, and he'd hide behind a tree and jump out and push everyone over. I'd tackle him, and we'd all wind up in a big pile, freezing, laughing, stuffed from the big meal.

NEW YEAR'S EVE

I'm not a big fan of New Year's. Everyone tries so hard to have a good time and winds up driving drunk, doing drugs, and spending hundreds of dollars on special menus because of the date on the calendar. The day before, you could eat the same food and drink the same wine at half the price, without the pressure of "the best night ever" and idiots going crazy up and down the avenues, puking and having sex in public. No, thank you.

We kept our celebration simple. First, we'd have a cake and a song for Don's birthday in the suite, and then Donald and I would go to dinner or a nightclub until midnight. Donald never drank a drop, and I would have only two glasses of champagne. Even in a gorgeous spot like Aspen, it wasn't a lot of fun to watch people drink themselves sloppy and stupid. We'd be back in our suite by twelve fifteen a.m.

EASTER

Spring break was always in Palm Beach. My parents would fly in for a few months, which was a cause for celebration for the kids. Depending on the year, some members of the Trump family would join us at Mar-a-Lago, too. Donald's sisters might bring their families, and we'd have fun in the ocean and lay out by the pool.

The day before Easter, the chef would make dozens of hardboiled eggs for the kids to color and paint. Then, on Easter Sunday morning, I'd sneak off and hide the eggs around the pool and the patio. The kids would run around like headless chickens to find those eggs, making it a competition (of course). Whoever found the most would win.

One year, I hid the eggs as usual in some very clever places—in the swan sculptures by the pool, under a bush by the lounge chairs. When I finished, I went back inside and said, "Okay, kids! Go!" It was like releasing the hounds. They took their baskets and ran straight to where I'd hid the eggs, as if they already knew exactly where to look. I found out later that as soon as I took the eggs to the pool to hide, the kids ran into the security room, where we had dozens of cameras monitoring every inch of the property. They watched me hiding the eggs the whole time! Those kids were too smart for their own good.

MOTHER'S DAY

Another Greenwich holiday, made special for me because my mother was always with us. The kids would make cards and little presents—drawings, bouquets of spring flowers picked from the garden, fresh-baked cookies—for Babi and me. The man in my life at the time would give me roses or orchids, which are always welcome. For dinner, we'd go to Manero's for lobster and steak to end my day on a delicious note.

HELICOPTER PARENTING, TRUMP-STYLE

I didn't choose to be a working mother. I *had* to work. I *needed* to work. If you are raised to push yourself to achieve bigger and tougher goals, you don't just stop doing that if you suddenly have enough money to sit on your butt and eat bonbons all day long. Not to say stay-at-home moms have it easy or don't work hard! My daughter-in-law Vanessa does more in one day than anyone I know. But the work I felt compelled to tackle was outside the home and in the business world. The same drive that made me a champion and propelled me out of Czechoslovakia was still firmly in place after I got married and had children. By working, I was true to myself. I taught my children about ambition and integrity as a living example. My professional goal was perfection, in the big picture and in every tiny detail. My children grew up watching me excel, and now I watch each one of them do exactly the same thing.

I fully acknowledge that my "having it all" was made possible by the help and support of my parents, the invaluable Bridget and Dorothy, and our incredible household staff, including David, my houseman for many years. Hillary Clinton wrote, "It takes a village to raise a child," which is one of the only things she's ever said that I wholeheartedly agree with.

ERIC

Both of my parents worked very hard and couldn't be there for us 24/7, so they filled those voids with people like Dorothy, Bridget, Vinnie, and Frank—Don's and my bosses at the construction site—and Tim, who worked for our family in Florida. Dorothy has never said a bad word about anyone in her life. She is pure and proper. I wouldn't call Vinnie and Frank pure and proper, just amazing, hardworking people. Tim was ex-military, a tough taskmaster. We always had incredible people around us who watched out for us when our parents couldn't be there themselves. My parents deserve a lot of credit for putting those positive influences in place.

Occasionally, when rushing to work on a Sunday, or having to interrupt vacations for a conference call, I had moments of doubt and wondered if I should lighten the workload to spend more time with the kids. But then I'd get into the flow at work and feel the laser focus when making decisions and taking care of business, really enjoying what I was doing, and think, *I'm great at this. I should be doing this. The kids are fine.* Maybe they would have liked me at home more often. But, then again, if I'd had to pour all of my energy and drive into being a stay-at-home mom, they may have wished I'd leave them alone and go get a job! I was the best mom I could be by being true to myself, and that meant having a demanding career.

I didn't hover over my kids, what people call "helicopter parenting." My version of helicopter parenting was to bring the kids to work with me in the Trump chopper. Why separate your two lives—career and family—if you can combine them? At least once a week, starting when they were very young, my kids saw firsthand how I operated at the office, and how I inspired and nurtured the dedication and loyalty of my employees. You can't force someone to respect you, especially when you're the wife of the owner. You have to earn it in your actions. I learned the business by listening to Donald—to be a tough negotiator, trust my gut, and value and reward loyalty—and the kids learned it by listening to both of us.

After we opened the Grand Hyatt, right on schedule, in 1980, my next job was to be the boss of hundreds of workers in the design and branding of Trump Tower on Fifth Avenue between Fifty-Sixth and Fifty-Seventh Streets, which became the home base for the Trump Organization and our family's home in the triplex penthouse overlooking Central Park. I picked out every piece of marble and every golden fixture in the place. The famous fountain in the lobby? My idea. The steel-and-glass façade? I pushed for that. I wanted the building that bore our name to be a modern marvel, to change the skyline of New York, and it did.

Onward! In 1984, I became the president and CEO of the Trump Castle Hotel and Casino, a from-the-ground-up construction of a luxury resort in Atlantic City that was located 130 miles from home. I was the first and only woman president and CEO of a major casino and oversaw a workforce of thousands, from the builders to the plumbers and electricians, housekeepers, pit bosses, croupiers, bartenders, entertainers, and bookers. You can't be a pussycat running a casino in New Jersey. I was tough but fair, and my employees loved me. The hotel launched in 1985. On any given day, thirty thousand people would be in and out the doors. The five-thousand-space car garage was always full.

Being president of a casino wasn't a Monday-to-Friday, nine-to-five job. The high rollers came on the weekends with wives or mistresses or both, and I had to be there to make sure they got the full treatment. Tickets to Sinatra, spots at high-stakes tables, all the lobster they could eat and Johnnie Walker Black they could drink. While the husbands and "uncles" gambled, their wives and "nieces" were kept occupied at the fashion shows and spa days that I organized for them.

I once asked a high roller, the owner of a toilet seat manufacturing company from Oklahoma, "Why do you do it? Why drop a fortune at the tables?"

He said, "Ivana, you have your house in Saint-Tropez, your yacht, a plane. You spend your money the way you want to. I'm happy at Trump Castle. You send a plane for me and pick me up at the airport in a limo. I have a host"—a host is a kind of nanny for adults who takes care of the high roller's every need—"I see the top shows and gamble. This is what I enjoy and how I want to spend my money."

He could afford it. Other players would lose their house, watch, car, cat, and dog in the process. A gambler might win two million in the morning and lose three million that night. In the end, the house always wins. Working at a casino taught me never to throw my money away. As the holder of a casino license, it's illegal for me to gamble (except in very particular parameters), but I wouldn't anyway. I enjoy playing blackjack and I happen to be very good at it, but I work too hard for my money to bet with it. None of my kids gamble, either.

On these weekly impromptu "take your kids to work" days at Trump Castle, I'd bring them to my office. While I cleared my desk, they'd drink soda and have snacks on the carpet. Every Friday night, my assistant would bring me a huge basket of checks to sign. There were automatic payroll checks for my four thousand employees, but I signed a thousand checks a week for food and liquor, restaurant and office supplies, you name it. I'd go over every requisition order with my vice president of purchasing and ask, "Why are they asking for another thousand decks of cards?" Every penny had to be justified and approved by me personally before I signed the check. The kids witnessed this process often.

On Saturdays, we'd explore the hotel and casino, go to the pool, have a buffet lunch, and watch *City Lights*, the ice-skating show. The kids were having a great time, but I was always working. Was the pool area clean? Were there enough towels? Was the buffet fully stocked? Was the ice show as entertaining as it could be? Ivanka called Trump Castle her own magical playground. Don was attracted to the boats and yachts in the marina. When he was thirteen, he was old enough to work there as a dockhand, helping people get to and from their boats, carrying luggage.

Another part of the business of running a hotel and casino was all the events—the concerts and conventions, boxing matches and trade shows. I exposed the kids to what was appropriate for them and shielded them from the unseemly. It was a balancing act of sharing the good (like a Diana Ross concert) and protecting them from the bad.

For example, in 1988, we organized and hosted the Mike Tyson and Michael Spinks prizefight at the Atlantic City Convention Hall next to the Trump Plaza Hotel and Casino. It was big business for us. The high rollers would come, stay in the hotel, and gamble until six a.m. The casino would make four times as much as whatever we paid the fighters. The Spinks/Tyson fight was promoted by Don King, an ostentatious man with supremely high eighties hair. When I met him, I had only one question: "What mousse do you use?" King did a masterful job of hyping the fight. Big celebrities—Madonna, Sean Penn, Sly Stallone, Oprah, Jack Nicholson, Warren Beatty, and Jesse Jackson, among others—sat in the front row with Donald, the kids, my father, Fred Trump, and me. The fight was short and bloody. No one screamed louder than Ivanka.

The kids never saw the behind-the-scenes ugliness of dealing with Mike Tyson. He came with an entourage of forty, and they ate insane quantities of pasta and steaks, and guzzled booze like there was no tomorrow. Mike and his wife, Robin Givens, stayed in a luxury suite next to mine. One morning, I met Robin in her suite and she had a huge black eye and was covered with bruises.

"What happened?" I asked.

"Michael got crazy last night and he bumped me off all four walls," she said.

Tyson came out of the bedroom and I said, "What's wrong with you? You can't treat her like that."

He just shrugged and said, "She pissed me off. Maybe I was drunk."

We never had him in the casino again. I was relieved when Robin outed his abuse soon after and divorced him. He was absolutely crazy.

Frank Sinatra used to sing in my casino four weekends a year and I took the kids to see him many times. But I made sure they didn't spend time with him because he was a terrible man.

Donald once had a meeting with Prince Rainier in Monaco. Barbara Sinatra heard that we were also staying at the Hôtel de Paris and called to invite us to dinner at the Grill with her and Frank, and Roger Moore, his wife, Luisa, and his daughter. This was during the Reagan era, and Frank was very friendly with Ron and Nancy. Barbara, not so much. At White House dinners, Mrs. Reagan would seat Barbara in Siberia (at a table far away from the action) and park Frank right next to her. At the Grill dinner, the Sinatras, Moores, Donald, and I were discussing the current war in Afghanistan, and Barbara made a critical comment about Reagan. Frank exploded. He jumped out of his chair and started *screaming* at her. "You're just a woman! You don't know anything! How dare you talk about my friend Ron that way?!"

I shrunk down and so did Donald. He looked at me across the table and he said, "And you thought I was bad!"

If that wasn't awful enough, later on that night, Frank insisted we all go down to the piano bar. When the elevator opened in the lobby, a just-married American couple—she was in her wedding gown and veil, and he in his tux—saw Frank and freaked out. She said, "Oh, Mr. Sinatra, we love you so much . . ."

Frank looked over his shoulder at his bodyguards and said, "Get rid of the bums."

The look on their faces! The couple was just destroyed. He could have said hello and shaken their hands. They didn't even have a camera. But he didn't because he was a mean bastard. I never hired him or spoke to him again.

I left my position at Trump Castle on a high note in 1987. My thousands of employees lined up on either side of the casino floor, cheering and applauding. I had no idea they were going to give me a standing ovation on my way out of the building! I was very touched and grateful to them. It warmed my heart that they felt the same way about me and I almost cried. But I had a new mountain to climb. Donald had given me my toughest job yet, appointing me president and CEO of the Plaza Hotel on Fifth Avenue between Fifty-Eighth and Fifty-Ninth Streets from 1987 to 1991. My commute was a lot easier, only a few blocks, but the work was even more intense. The Plaza was a New York landmark, known for its elegance and old-world charm. Thus far, my specialty was modern construction, glass and chrome, but the new Plaza had to be respectful of its long history. I managed a staff of 1,400 people and kept them on their toes. Sometimes, I'd stand at my window in Trump Tower and watch the entrance of the Plaza through binoculars. If luggage was left outside for too long, or there was garbage out front, I'd call over there and get it taken care of immediately. The Plaza hosted hundreds of major fashion shows, weddings, black-tie parties, and business conferences every year. I presided over all of them, and dressed fabulously doing it.

When I moved to the Plaza, it was a lot easier to bring the kids to work with me, and they were in my office constantly. Ivanka roamed the Plaza at will—the ballrooms, kitchens, and restaurants. The staffers called her a modern-day Eloise.

She particularly enjoyed joining me on site inspections. I'd block off one floor per week and take it out of business. No bookings at all for seven days. Then I'd go room to room with the vice president of housekeeping, maid, electrician, painter, and plumber. In room 901, for example, I might notice a crack in the paint, some peeling caulk around the toilet, mismatched hangers in the closet. Every room and common area was gone over with a fine-tooth comb, and everything I said was recorded. Was the paint fresh? Were the corridor sand ashtrays cleaned and groomed? I'd re-teach the maids how to turn down the bed, fold and hang the towels. If a maid or maintenance staffer didn't make the changes I asked for, they got a warning. After three warnings, they were gone. I walked through the hotel for three hours every day, and Ivanka was right there at my side, soaking it in.

For lunch, I took her to the Palm Court, where ladies in hats and gloves had high tea. I'd take her to catering and we'd ask the chef to present an upcoming wedding menu and service for us. They'd put together the whole table, from the china pattern to the flowers, and Ivanka and I would sample the food, from appetizers to dessert, and talk about what to keep and what to change.

Far more important than which napkins go with what flatware were workplace morals and etiquette. Ivanka learned, by watching me interact with people, to be polite *always* and treat everyone with the same level of respect. It didn't matter if I was talking to the dishwasher or a vice president. We were on the same team and proud of it. I never asked anyone to do something they couldn't do, but I expected the best from everyone. The very first thing I did was to expand and improve the employee cafeteria. I gave them beautiful new uniforms and upgraded their equipment, from vacuums to computers. I started my job by making my team happy. They would have killed for me, and I for them.

On the wall of my office at the Plaza, I had a framed check in the amount of one dollar, written out to me by Donald. When it was announced that I was going to run the Plaza, a reporter asked him about my salary, and he said, "One dollar and all the dresses she can wear." He had no idea how many dresses I could wear in a year—or how much they cost! He meant it as a joke, but people accused him of being sexist. The truth is, I wasn't working for a salary. The Trump Organization was, and is, a family company, and I was part of the family. We were partners in marriage and in business. Whatever we had, we shared. That was my principle, and I framed and hung the check as a symbol of that. Anyone who doubted my leadership or hotelier skills and thought I got my jobs just because of my relationship with Donald should have walked for one day in my stilettos. I *earned* my positions and the respect of my staffs every day as a point of pride.

Back to those dresses . . . My job included looking glamorous at all the weddings, fashion shows, and events I hosted, and that did require quite a number of haute couture dresses. I went to Fashion Weeks in Milan, Paris, London, and New York every year, before and after the divorce. In the eighties, my father would meet me in

Paris and he'd be my date at the shows and after-parties. People would look at me dancing with a very handsome older man, and tongues would wag. Ivanka started coming along with me when she was six or seven. She might not remember, but she saw Calvin Klein, Ungaro, Todd Oldham, and Versace collections while sitting on my lap. In Paris, twenty-five of my girlfriends and I would stay at Hôtel Plaza Athénée, have lunches and dinners, and go to the shows every season. Eight-year-old Ivanka would sit next to socialite Nan Kempner; Pat Buckley, the wife of William F. Buckley Jr.; or Jerry Zipkin, and talk about Dior and Givenchy.

In the early nineties, soon after the divorce, the kids; my second husband, Riccardo; and I spent a month cruising around Greece on his yacht and visiting Aristotle Onassis's island, Skorpios, and we stayed for a few weeks in a villa in Lefkada, next to Corfu. We hadn't gone public as a couple yet and were trying to keep it quiet. He decided he wanted tuna sandwiches for lunch one day, so I went into a tiny store to buy a few cans. While I was paying, the grocer looked at me and said, "You look like that wealthy American woman. Ivana."

I said, "I wish I had her money!" and ran out.

The villa was lovely, with a maid and butler. I brought my own sheets, posters for the walls, napkins, and cutlery. I had twenty pieces of luggage to take with me from Greece to France to see the haute couture collections. Somewhere along the way from Athens to Frankfurt to Paris, my luggage got lost. Lufthansa had no idea where any of it was. Ivanka, ten at the time, and I were supposed to be at a Valentino show in two hours, but we had nothing to wear. Thankfully, Valentino came to my rescue and gave me a dress. For Ivanka, I took the Versace blouse and skirt I was wearing on the plane, rolled up the sleeves and waist, and pinned the garments to fit. As we were leaving our hotel for the show, Gianni Versace saw us, came over, and said, "I didn't know I was making children's clothes!"

I left the Plaza in 1991, and at forty-one, I went into business for myself. Divorce didn't break my spirit. If anything, I was determined to create a great life for us by making my own money, showing the children that we could survive anything, even the dismantling of our family. I started a new career that allowed me to work from home, at least part of the time, and continued to involve the kids in my professional life.

I opened Ivana Inc., with offices at 501 Park Avenue, the arm of my business that pertained to my books, advice columns, commercials (Pizza Hut, Got Milk?, and Kentucky Fried Chicken, to name a few), appearances, and lectures. The other arm of my business was the House of Ivana fragrances, clothes, and jewelry that sold like wildfire on home shopping networks in three countries.

A lot of people have asked me about the home shopping channel process. Let me break it down for you:

First, I worked with designers, picking out fabrics and making sketches. Every month, we'd make a hundred samples. Racks of clothing and boxes of jewelry would come to my home or office for my personal inspection. I'd make sure every button, every zipper, was exactly the way I wanted it, and if not, it went back out to be changed. I was on top of every detail. It was like working at the Plaza and scrutinizing the table settings, but with fabric and jewels.

Then three buyers from three networks would come to see a

once-a-month presentation of the samples. First, the Canadian buyer would come, and she'd say, "I'll take five thousand of these rings and five thousand of these tops," and so on. Then the American buyer would come and place even bigger orders, and lastly, the British buyer. The United Kingdom was a tough market. European women like to pick out their scarves at Hermès and don't want to buy something on TV. After taking a risk on their first purchases, though, my customers learned to trust the quality of my products, especially my jewelry, clothing, and face creams. The hardest sell? Fragrance. It's very personal. People need to smell it on their own skin. After the presentations, I'd send the buy orders to the factories. Once the products were made, they went through network quality control.

Finally, I'd sell the merchandise. The first weekend of every month, I'd be at HSN in Tampa, Florida. I'd leave New York on Thursday morning and was on the air Thursday evening starting at six p.m. I'd sell for two hours, take an hour off, go back on the air for an hour, take an hour off, etc., until midnight, or later. And then I'd do it again on Friday and Saturday. By Sunday, I couldn't stand the sound of my own voice. Monday through Wednesday were devoted to approving new collections. On the second weekend of every month, I'd fly to Canada for another six-hours-on-air, three-days-in-a-row schedule at TSN. The third weekend, I went to London QVC to do it all over again. The fourth weekend was free.

I kept up this cycle of designing, manufacturing, and selling at a breakneck pace for *nineteen years*. What can I say? I like to make money. I could sell $3 million in a weekend. The price points were low—say, from $49 for a blouse to $199 for a suit. Priced to sell, and man, did they ever. I'd move five thousand bottles of perfume in an evening. My sales record was $675,000 in one hour. If I didn't sell $200,000 an hour, it was a disappointment. I absolutely had something to prove. I could earn a fabulous living on my own, using just my first name.

"Ivana" was on every garment and bauble, so the quality had to be excellent. I couldn't go on TV and sell something I didn't believe in. Some celebrities do their infomercials and say, "Isn't this face cream fantastic?" when they haven't even tried it or wouldn't be caught dead using it. Not me. I used my products and wore my merchandise. My fellow home shopping pioneer presenter Joan Rivers felt the same way. She loved her brands and wore her jewelry and makeup every day. Joan lived only a couple of blocks away from me on the Upper East Side. I rooted for her when she appeared on *The Celebrity Apprentice* and was thrilled when she won. She was a great, funny woman. I miss her.

While House of Ivana was getting off the ground, Ivanka watched the whole soup-to-nuts process: how a lizard pin, for example, went from idea, to sample, into mass production, and finally onto the lapels of a hundred thousand women around the world. She weighed in at the designer presentations and gave her "It's cute!" or "Not feeling it" opinions, which I took very seriously.

She saw me branding for years and years back in the days when TV shopping and celebrity lines were new concepts. While I was still on the air, Ivanka, then twenty-six, launched her own jewelry line. I would go on my shows selling silver hoop earrings for $49.99, and she'd sell a similar pair—hers were crusted in diamonds—at her boutique on Madison Avenue for $38,000. My brand was mass-market and hers was luxury. Different markets, but we shared a commitment to quality. She knew not to put her name on a product she didn't believe in completely. Would she have been so brand savvy if she hadn't grown up watching me create my lines from scratch? Who knows?

IVANKA

Unlike a lot of parents who are passionate about their professions but keep home and career separate, Mom incorporated us into every aspect of her life. Not many kids sat on the floor of their mother's office while she was on the phone, tagged along on site inspections, got to go with her to lunch with her friends, or greeted guests when she entertained. She led by example and taught me how to conduct myself in all these realms. Some of my friends' parents tried to instruct their kids about business or socializing by sitting them down for a lecture. Mom allowed us to flourish and learn from watching her, listening to her conversations, and seeing how she handled herself.

EVERYTHING BUT THE CAT

I'm a dog person, through and through. My childhood dog, Brok, was the big brother I never had. I can't imagine a childhood without a pet of some kind. From animals, people get a pure, unconditional love. When a dog wags his tail and licks your face, all the stress and pressure of life goes away. How can you not love a dog that acts like he's won the lottery for life just because he sees you walk through the door?

I've told you about Chappy and his deep love for my chinchilla coat. He had an equal dislike of Donald. Whenever Donald went near my closet, Chappy would bark at him territorially. Despite their issues with each other, Donald never objected to Chappy's sleeping on my side of the bed.

The kids adored Chappy, of course. Even when he smelled bad.

My mother, Ivanka, and I used to take long walks in the woods with the dog when my father and the boys were fishing. One day, we came upon a beautiful little creature as it ran out of a bush. It had a silky black coat, and we thought it was a mink or an otter. When the animal saw us, it stopped, and then turned around. I noticed the white stripe on its back, and then the skunk lifted its tail. I said, "Run!" My daughter, my mother, and I sprinted away and got far enough away not to be sprayed. Chappy wasn't so lucky. He came home a few minutes later smelling like death. As clean and well groomed as he was, Chappy had very thick, curly black hair, and the stench clung to every strand of it. The kids and I gave him a bath in two gallons of tomato juice, which made him smell like death that'd been rolled through an Italian restaurant. Chappy was not allowed to sleep on my fur coats or sit on the couches for a few weeks. Other than that, he didn't seem to mind his skunk encounter at all. In fact, he always sniffed around that bush, like he was hoping to see his smelly friend again.

Dodo, a Yorkie, came into our lives after the divorce. Riccardo and I were dating, and he was getting to know the kids. He went to a pet store on Lexington and Sixty-Second Street, picked out the tiniest, cutest little puppy in the store, and brought Dodo home in the pocket of his coat. He said to Eric and Ivanka (Don was away at boarding school), "I've got a surprise for you." He put his hand in his pocket and held out Dodo, who was small enough to sit on his open palm. The kids went nuts! They were delighted and immediately started to fight over who got to hold the puppy. Chappy was an old man by then, but he and Dodo got along very well and they kept each other company. Dodo was just a sweetheart, full of love and energy. He wasn't very bright, but that made him even more adorable. I thought of Chappy as the wise one. Dodo ran around in circles.

Chappy lived to be sixteen. In his final years, he put on a lot of weight. He could hardly walk and had lost control of his bladder. He started to sleep in the basement laundry room in Greenwich because he couldn't walk up the stairs. It was heartbreaking to see him struggle with everything. We loved him, but it was time. I took him to the vet and Chappy was put to sleep. We dug a hole on a hill at the edge of the property near a very old headstone—it was so old and faded, I have no idea whose stone it was; it could have been from two hundred years ago—and put Chappy to rest. At the burial, we all cried and were upset. It wasn't my style to turn his death into a teachable moment. It was just a time to be sad and to appreciate how much he meant to us, to be grateful for the memories, and then to let him go. We said our good-byes at the grave site and then we went back inside for lunch.

Along with the dogs, we had tropical fish, turtles, hamsters, a rabbit that smelled horrible, and a pair of parakeets. We took the birds with us to Greenwich on the weekends in their cage. After one drive, I carried the cage into the house and noticed that one of the parakeets was lying stiff on the bottom of the cage. I didn't want the kids to know, so the next day, I went to the village pet store in Greenwich and bought a look-alike replacement. Ivanka and Eric had no idea. Don took one look in the cage and said, "That is *not* our parakeet!"

The only time I said no to a household pet was when the kids wanted a cat. They shed and scratch furniture. No way was I going to allow one of them anywhere near my damask couches! I think cats are beautiful, but at the end of the day, I'm a dog person.

One year, Don or Eric brought home a white mouse from school at the end of the year and begged me to let him keep her. Over my dead body would I allow a rodent in Trump Tower! "The hamsters are rodents, too!" Don said, as we'd had some of those. He was absolutely right. Hamsters are rodents and I allowed two of them to live in a glass tank in Trump Tower. For whatever reason, hamsters seemed okay, like pets, while mice were *not* okay. Maybe it has something to do with the long twitchy nose, hairless pink tail, and glowing red devil eyes.

We compromised on Greenwich, but only if the mouse lived in a cage in the garage. The kids set up a beautiful home for the mouse and spent whole days in the garage playing with her. The grounds-keeper fed her whenever we weren't there. As soon as we arrived at the house on Friday, the kids ran straight out there to see her. After about a month, they brought the cage into the house and made me look. Inside, there were a dozen baby mice, white with red bulging eyes.

I screamed, "Get them out of here!" If one got loose, I'd be chasing mice all over the house forever. Sure enough, one of them did get out of the cage, and Patrick the houseman and the kids were scurrying around trying to catch it. Thank God they were able to find it on the carpet. The house was huge, fifty thousand square feet. If they hadn't caught it, we'd have wound up sharing the place with thousands of the critters. That one daring escape was all I could handle. As soon as school started again in the fall, the mice went back.

We adopted a stray duck once, too. We found him in Greenwich

on the side of the road. The kids named him Wobbly and he followed us everywhere. He did wobble pathetically because he had
a damaged leg, and I'm pretty sure he'd been hit in the head. We
took him to our vet, who made Wobbly well. While he healed, he
had a cushy month in Don's bathtub. When he seemed good to
go, we took him to the pond by the house and said, "Fly! Be free!"
but Wobbly wasn't going anywhere. He insisted on following us
around, on walks, to the beach, right alongside the dog. Eventually,
Wobbly gave in to the call of the wild and flew away. I can only
imagine the stories he told the other ducks about us.

My last poodle was also named Chappy, also black, and just as sweet
as his predecessor. He nearly gave me a heart attack in 2000 when
he escaped the town house when a florist came to deliver flowers. My boyfriend at the time, Roffredo Gaetani, and I searched
high and low for him in Central Park and up and down the avenues, calling his name for hours. I put up dog posters offering a
thousand-dollar reward all over the neighborhood, frantically asking everyone if they'd seen him. I called the police, the *New York
Post*, anyone and everyone who could help me find him.

In the afternoon, the doorbell rang. I ran to open it, and there
was Chappy, in the arms of a doorman from my veterinarian's building! I was thrilled and so relieved. "How did you find him?" I asked.

Apparently, Chappy was initially found on Park Avenue by a
dog walker, who brought him to a nearby building and handed him
off to two doormen. They took care of him for a few hours before
they delivered him to the nearest veterinarian, who happened to be
Lewis Berman, my own vet. Since Chappy wasn't wearing his collar,

Dr. Berman didn't recognize him at first, but then his receptionist went to get some lunch and saw my posters. The next thing I knew, my vet's doorman had brought Chappy home to me. I couldn't track down the dog walker, but I gave $1,000 each to the doormen. One made a dent in the reward by taking his wife out to a very nice dinner, and the other one gave his reward money to charity.

From that day forward, Chappy wore his collar no matter what. We got very lucky that day. The combination of the posters, spreading the word, and having kind neighbors made our one-in-a-million reunion possible. New York may seem like a big, scary city, but in many ways, it's a small town.

My last dog to date was Tiger, a Yorkie. He was slightly more intelligent than Dodo and just as freaking adorable. We were constant companions for eleven years. When I got my hair done, Tiger went to his doggie salon. When I went for a checkup, Tiger saw the vet. When I flew first-class to the South of France, Tiger sat right next to me in his carrier or on the seat and was an absolute champ about never peeing on the plane or inside the airport. I don't know how he could hold it for ten hours, but he did. Such a good boy!

Of the three kids, Eric followed in my footsteps to become a through-and-through dog person. He and his wife, Lara, adopted a miniature beagle named Charlie from a rescue, and they dote on him. Eric wasn't so sure if they would adopt at first because he spends so much time on planes away from home, but Lara convinced him, and Eric fell instantly in love with Charlie, whose tail is always wagging. He's their little baby, and they post photos of him on social media constantly. Charlie has a new brother, Ben, a full-size beagle with a beautiful face, recently adopted from a rescue. When Ben arrived at the shelter, he was in terrible shape. He'd been abused and was afraid of people, especially men. I think their original idea was to foster Ben to socialize him before helping place him with another family. But you know what happens when you live with a dog that gazes up at you with those big brown eyes. He only wants two things: affection and food. It's a pure relationship and you can't help but fall in love. Eric and Lara worked to gain Ben's trust, and now he's doing fabulously well. He and Charlie are best friends and they're a family of four—soon to be five! Eric and Lara are expecting their first child in September 2017.

Don has two Havanese, a toy breed, that he calls "little monsters." His house, with five kids and two yapping dogs, is a happy chaos.

Ivanka is holding off on getting a dog just yet, but I think she'll come around soon. Her kids can be very persuasive, just like she was at their age.

PART FOUR

SURVIVING THE WORST OF THE WORST

HOLDING US TOGETHER

I'd heard some whispers.

Cindy Adams had asked me if the rumors were true, that Donald was cheating on me, at a party at the Waldorf Astoria the week before. I was so angry that she'd even suggest it that I didn't speak to her again for years. Apart from gossip, which you always have to take with a kilo of salt, I had no reason to suspect him of straying. Donald hadn't lost weight or changed his hair. He wasn't dressing better or making mysterious charges on the credit cards. He acted exactly the same as he always had at home.

On December 30, 1989, the day before Don turned twelve, Donald, the kids, and I were in Aspen, having lunch at Bonnie's, a popular restaurant at the ski resort, when this young blond woman came up to me out of the blue and said, "I'm Marla and I love your husband. Do you?"

I said, "Get lost. I love my husband."

It was unladylike, but I was in shock.

The kids were next to me on the food line, watching the whole exchange. My heart sank into my ski boots. All three have since told me that they barely registered this confrontation with the interloper, but later that night, they must have heard Donald and me fighting back at the chalet. We'd originally planned to stay in Aspen for another few days, but my instincts told me to run, to get far away from the place where my life had turned upside down, the same impulse that sent me out of Czechoslovakia after Jiří died.

The press knew about the confrontation at Bonnie's—many people were there to see it and the gossip was spreading—and were watching our every move. We decided to return home when originally planned and act as if everything was normal. I was very careful around the kids, but they definitely sensed that I was upset and were affectionate with me to cheer me up. When Eric gave me a hug or Ivanka held my hand, I struggled to control my emotions. I was shattered and shocked. Putting on a brave front for the kids during those first few days was one of the hardest things I've ever done.

Back in New York in January 1990, Donald and I slept in the same bed, watched TV together, and talked about work. He would try to put his arm around me, but I wouldn't let him. I didn't file for divorce until March, but as far as I was concerned, the marriage ended that day at Bonnie's. How could I continue if every time he said he was going to play golf, my first thought would be, *Is he lying? Is he meeting someone?* I couldn't live like that. After fourteen

years, countless challenges and triumphs, three children, and so
much love, our marriage was over.

Looking back at the first year after the split, I can only shake my
head about how insane it was. The media tsunami put my private
sorrow on the front page of the *Daily News* and *New York Post* for
ninety days in a row. "Trump vs. Trump" was the longest-running
front-page story in tabloid history until O. J. Simpson led cops on
a low-speed car chase a few years later.

The headlines were poisoned arrows: "Split!" "Love on the
Rocks!" "They Met in Church," "Separate Beds," and the topper,
"The Best Sex I Ever Had." Every day, a mob of reporters camped
outside Trump Tower. They hounded my children at their schools
and at friends' houses. I couldn't turn on the television without
hearing my name. "Ivana" had been synonymous with glamour,
elegance, and success. And then, for a time, it was associated only
with being a cheated-upon wife.

Through it all, I had faith in myself. I was mentally tough and
I knew I'd survive. But the destruction of my marriage wasn't only
about me. I had to guide Don, twelve; Ivanka, eight; and Eric, six,
through a firestorm that no one could have imagined or prepared
for. But we were in it, and I had to come up with a plan to get myself
and my children through this nightmare with minimal emotional
damage.

I made two rules for myself: (1) Never show panic in front of
the kids. If they saw me fall apart, they would, too. Of course, I was
vulnerable and heartbroken. There were very dark moments, and
sometimes, I just wanted to scream. But I always waited until I was

alone, or with my mother and father, to cry. (2) Never speak a bad word about Donald. Even an eye roll or a strange look would send the wrong message. No matter what my husband had done to me, he was still their father. The children had happy memories of our life together, and one angry word from me could make them see our history in a different light. My goal was to keep their love for me *and* for him intact, no matter how I felt about Donald at the time. Thinking long-term was extremely difficult while suffering in the moment, but I'd seen how badly friends of mine had handled their divorces with the kids. I didn't want that to happen to us.

Guided by my two rules, I got us through a 24/7 living nightmare that didn't let up for a year. I didn't create the chaos that my separation caused, but I did confront it by being firmly in control of my behavior at all times. Divorce is never easy for children. It's a disaster every time. But my family came out of an excruciating split just fine, which I consider one of my greatest accomplishments as a parent.

How did I pull off that miracle? Day by day, dignity came first.

I had to tell the children what was going on before they heard about it from someone else. It was agony to speak about what was happening, even to my friends, and talking about my heartbreak to the kids would only happen if I stuck to the facts. I focused on the goals of avoiding drama (no slamming doors or raised voices in my home *ever*) and reassuring them that everything was going to be okay.

I spoke to each child separately. I told Eric, "Your father is not living with us anymore. He's moving to another apartment, his parents' one on the twenty-ninth floor. I'm still your mother and he'll always be your father. You can see him anytime you want." Eric accepted the news. He probably had questions, but when I first explained the situation, he just went back to what he was playing with.

Don was old enough to want to know more, and, after careful consideration, I decided he could handle hearing the truth. I kept my feelings in check and said, "Your father had a mistress and I can't be with him anymore. We've decided to live apart and get a divorce. But you're not divorcing him. I am." Don was protective of me. After that initial talk, he took it upon himself to monitor my feelings. He always asked how I was, hugged me, and stayed up late with me. He was furious with his father and didn't speak to him for a year. The last thing he said to Donald, before icing him out, was "How can you say you love us? You don't love us! If you loved us, you wouldn't have done this."

Ivanka had friends with divorced parents, so she understood the concept, but she was still very young and there was no reason to air her father's dirty laundry. She got the same speech as Eric. Her only question was "Is there any chance you'll make up?" It was hard for her to understand what was going on. After all, Donald and I didn't fight and there was never tension around the dinner table or on vacations (until Aspen). From her perspective, we were a close, happy family. I felt just as blindsided as she did.

I said, "I'm sorry, sweetheart. But your father and I will never get back together."

To me, loyalty is the most important quality in a person, and trust is the most valuable asset in a marriage. If the trust is broken, the marriage is finished. I have never wavered on that. I know many people stay in bad marriages because they think it'll be good for the kids. Others feel their children would have a better chance with happy parents who live apart than miserable parents together.

Nowadays, I look at political wives who stand by their cheating, lying husbands at press conferences with a glazed look in their eyes, and I can't believe they put up with it. How do they explain it to their children? I'm thinking of one particular political wife who became a politician herself. Not too long after my divorce was finalized in 1992, I attended a speech given by Hillary Clinton. At the time, her husband's chronic unfaithfulness was all over the news, and it would get much worse before he left office. I went up to her and asked, "How do you deal with it?" She knew I was talking about the cheating. She just looked at me and walked away. I've often wondered what course her life would have taken if she'd left Bill after the Monica Lewinsky scandal.

The first thing Donald and I sorted out was that I would have sole custody of the children and that he would take them every other weekend. He continued to see them twice a day, once in the morning before school, and once in the evening, as usual. As far as the kids were concerned, the only change in their home life (besides the reporters camping out in front of the building) was that their father didn't sleep in my bed anymore. They were still in the same apartment, slept in the same bedrooms, played with the same toys, wore the same clothes, went to the same schools, rode in the same cars, and took the same vacations. Predictability gives children a sense of security. I also made sure that they understood their other relationships would not change. Bridget and Dorothy weren't going anywhere. Babi and Dedo would always be their grandparents and love them as much as ever. Our well-established routine would not waver. Staying busy and on schedule was the best therapy for them.

I shielded them from *a lot*. One day, while riding the private elevator going to our triplex, I noticed a security camera in the ceiling that hadn't been there the day before. I put a glob of Krazy Glue on the tip of an umbrella and smeared it on the lens. Every move I made was being watched by the doormen and security personnel, and reported back to the man who signed their paychecks. I'd experienced the same kind of scrutiny from the communists, and the triplex started to feel like a palatial prison. If anyone—whether they were friends or deliverymen—was coming to see me, I asked them to give their name to the Trump Tower concierge as Mr. or Mrs. Brown. I knew he'd been instructed to call Donald and report in about all of my visitors. Whenever I pictured Donald asking, "Who the hell is Mr. Brown?" I always smiled.

As I've said, loyalty is everything to me, and nothing hurt more than being stabbed in the back for money. In the midst of the divorce—at one of the lowest points of my life—someone who'd worked for me for eight years went to the press. I heard that she was paid $10,000 to sell me out. The next thing I knew, a tabloid was calling me the worst mother of the year.

We all know that fathers get a standing ovation for every teeny tiny thing they do for their kids, and mothers are barely acknowledged for moving mountains on a daily basis. I'd taken care of every aspect of the kids' lives since birth while working full-time at one Trump property or another. Donald loved his children, was affectionate, and was a good provider. He took them to Elton John concerts at Madison Square Garden or to Yankee Stadium to hang out with George Steinbrenner. But he'd be the first to admit that he had no idea how to engage the kids at their respective ages and converse on their level. The children didn't know how to relate to him, either. Ivanka always said that her big breakthrough with Donald happened when she was old enough to talk about business. Meanwhile, I'd been engaging, relating, working with, managing, and molding my children *all along*. I tried to ignore the papers, but that unfit-mother headline really got to me.

Don expressed his pain with anger, and he was *really* angry about the tabloid slamming me as a bad mother. He wanted to call the paper and tell them they were wrong and that their source lied. I sat him down and taught him a lesson he'd have to learn again and again: it's hard not to take the headlines personally, but you can't let them define you. I said, "You know who you are and who we are. The press is just noise."

Reassuring the kids became the third part of my survival plan, along with putting on a brave face and never trashing their father. I would sit them down, look them in the eye, smile, and say, "We're okay," and then wrap them in a big, safe hug. There were times when I didn't know if I was reassuring them or myself.

The day after the unfit-mother headline, Donald sent a body-guard to the triplex with instructions to bring Don—who was still not speaking to his father—down to his office on the twenty-eighth floor. I didn't think anything of it because the kids visited his office every day, so off Don went with the bodyguard.

A few minutes later, my husband called and said, "Ivana, I'm keeping Don. You're not getting him back. I'm going to bring him up myself."

"Okay, keep him," I said. "I have two other kids to raise."

Dead silence. He hung up, and ten minutes later, the bodyguard brought Don back. Donald never had any intention of keeping his son. It was a tactic to upset me. His plan backfired, though. I felt a bit stronger.

At home, I kept the TVs off and hid the papers and magazines from the kids to limit their exposure to the media onslaught, but they still had to walk through the gauntlet of reporters and photographers outside Trump Tower every day. They followed the kids to school, shouting inappropriate questions about the intimate lives of their parents. Some of Don's and Ivanka's classmates showed them newspapers and asked them what was happening at home.

There was an incident at Buckley, Don's school. The headmaster called me to say Don had gotten into a fight with two older students—and beaten the daylights out of them. Apparently, they'd said something unsavory about me to him. I told the headmaster that I don't approve of violence and would tell my son not to hit other kids. Privately, I was proud of him for defending me. To Don, I said punching wasn't the answer no matter how mean those boys were. It was better not to give them the satisfaction of knowing they'd gotten to him. Don took my advice to heart and never punched anyone again.

Eric was only six, too young to understand why there were reporters outside, but he felt the strange energy around the house, much as I tried to sweep it out. His kindergarten teacher called to tell me that three or four times a day, Eric, usually an eager, involved learner, would stare out the window and lose the thread of the lesson in the classroom. If he'd also stopped eating and sleeping well, I would have been alarmed and taken steps. But the teacher and I discussed it and decided it was normal for a child to check out for a bit, especially if there was a change at home. We watched him closely for any sign of real trouble. Fortunately, trouble never reared its head.

Ivanka was having a hard time at Chapin, too. Some mean girls teased her about the headlines, but she kept her head high and went about her business. Ivanka despised the reporters with a passion, but somehow, she didn't once reply to their relentless baiting. She wasn't angry with her father like Don was. In fact, she visited him in his office more often and played on the carpet for longer periods. She's said that after he moved out, she didn't take her father for granted anymore and made a point of spending more time with him.

With the army of reporters outside, I couldn't casually walk in and out of the main entrance to, say, take my dog for a walk. I had to sneak out through the loading dock. For my forty-first birthday, a few dozen of my friends threw a party for me on Valentine's Day at La Grenouille, a fantastic French restaurant at Fifth Avenue and East Fifty-Second Street. I was so touched by the show of support from Barbara Walters, Liz Smith, Nikki Haskell, Chessy Rayner, my sister-in-law Blaine Trump, and my mother-in-law, Mary Trump. The press got wind of the luncheon, and the street outside the restaurant was mobbed. Total mayhem. The police closed off the street. People were screaming my name and saying things like "Take him to the cleaners!" My bodyguards had to create a path for me to get to my car to leave. The crowd was definitely on my side, but I didn't take comfort in it. My family was destroyed. It was nothing to cheer about.

Columnist Liz Smith gave me great advice about how to

handle the media and recommended a publicist. With someone else fending off media requests (I didn't do a single interview for over a year), I could focus on my number one priority: maintaining a bubble of normalcy for the kids at home.

I read the columns and articles and I appreciated how many writers (and readers) of the press seemed to take my side. Liz's profile cast me as a symbol of female strength and dignity. "Ivana is now a media goddess on par with Princess Di, Madonna, and Elizabeth Taylor," she wrote. The praise was better than a punch in the stomach, but it didn't change the fact that my world had collapsed.

I never once played the victim. I have always been a fighter, faced whatever life threw at me head-on, and refused to sink into sadness, grief, or misery, no matter what happened. I would do it again this time, too, not only for my sake, but for my children. I was a Lion Mom who was prepared to do anything to protect her cubs.

Two days after my Valentine's Day birthday luncheon, the *Post* ran its infamous "The Best Sex I Ever Had" headline, accompanied by a story detailing what the showgirl apparently said about my husband, accompanied by a picture of Donald, smirking.

It was the last straw. Any semblance of "normal" was no longer possible. Before that day, a hundred photographers were following us. After that cover, it was a thousand, and they were pushier and more obnoxious than ever. The whole city of New York had gone crazy! For the physical and emotional safety of my children, we had to get out of town immediately and sequester ourselves. It was a few weeks before spring break. I figured I'd pull them out of school early and they'd just do their homework from a safe, private location and fax it in. But where could I go with Don, Ivanka, Eric, Babi, Dedo, Bridget, Dorothy, the dog, and all of our luggage without being swarmed?

I knew just the place.

I didn't make a big deal about it so as not to frighten the children. The staff and I just quietly, methodically moved our stuff out of Trump Tower, into cars, and to the airport. We got on a private plane and touched down in Palm Beach a few hours later. Mar-a-Lago is an enormous property with a private beach and excellent security. No one could get to us there, and I knew nothing upsetting could filter in if I didn't want it to. The kids would be totally insulated from the hysteria surrounding their parents. In our sanctuary, I upheld the "no crying, no drama" rule, and encouraged the kids to spend time in the sunshine, swim, play, and, of course, keep up with the homework assignments their teachers sent every morning.

In the past, our Mar-a-Lago retreat had always been alive with people running around and having fun. But that February and March, no one was allowed to come over, not even the kids' friends. I couldn't risk anybody talking about us, even to say we were fine and doing well. Providing grist for the gossip mill would defeat the purpose of our escape to Florida. None of our neighbors were invited over, either, although they knew we were there. Circling paparazzi helicopters were a dead giveaway.

I was very cautious about the household personnel, too. Only key staffers were kept on during those months. Even if something simple and innocent got out to the tabloids, it would have felt like a violation. The first couple of weeks in Palm Beach were difficult. I was reeling and struggled to keep up a brave face for the kids. My only emotional outlet was my parents. I spoke (and cried) only to them about my feelings. They were extremely angry at Donald, whom they'd always loved. As furious as they were, they upheld my rule not to bad-mouth him to the kids. I don't know what I would have done without their love and support. Being with them reminded me of what I'd already survived. I knew I'd be okay this time, too. I might have to downsize. So what? I could work and get a job outside the Trump Organization. I was smart and passionate; I could support myself and my kids if need be. My parents helped me focus my thoughts on what I had going for me, and my bedrock principles, instead of letting me spiral down into panic and misery. They kept saying, "You did nothing wrong." So why should I dwell on what I might've done differently in my marriage? I'd been a loyal, loving wife, and there was no reason to blame myself for what he did. I'd bounce back from this. One day, I'd be fine, I told myself. For now, I thought, *Don't sit around and think about things you can't change. Focus on being in control now, and in the future.*

For Don, Ivanka, and Eric, Mar-a-Lago was heaven. They knew why we were there to some extent, but as far as they were concerned, it was an unexpected vacation. They went swimming and played tennis every day, went to the beach, and spent a lot of time under the sun. My father took the kids fishing and my mother made incredible meals for us. I don't think the kids missed their friends because they had each other. They became a tight little unit in those months and took it to heart that they had to stick together, because, at the end of the day, family is all you've got. I think the bonding they did during the spring of 1990 cemented their closeness.

If the kids ever had a shaky moment or felt overwhelmed, I reminded them what really mattered. "Your father and I love you,"

I said. "That will never change." As complicated as divorce can be—
and mine was at the top of the all-time list—the explanations I
gave my kids were pretty simple. Were they safe? Did they feel
loved? Was it between the parents and not them? Yes, yes, and yes.
Even though I answered their questions about the state of my marriage, they were curious to know more. They knew I was holding
things back from them. A few times, I'd go into a room to take a
private phone call from a lawyer, and I'd hear sounds in the hallway.
I'd open the door to find the kids bent over like they'd had their
ears pressed against the wood. They were trying to spy on me! Once
caught, they ran away with Chappy chasing after them. It was hard
to believe that in such a large home, privacy was nearly impossible.
I issued an ironclad house rule: if I was in my room with the door
closed, no one was allowed to come in or to go anywhere near it.

My friends called constantly and sent letters and gifts to Florida, which I appreciated—but I didn't always call or write back. I
had to walk a very fine line with what I said, even to trusted allies.
I didn't want to be paranoid, but more people—a ski instructor,
one of my managers at the Plaza—were crawling out of the wood-
work to sell their stories about me to the press, and that made me
overly cautious. A select few friends came down, including Shirley
Lord. Shirley, a beauty editor at *Vogue*, convinced me to be on the
cover of the May 1990 issue of the magazine. Photographer Patrick Demarchelier and the *Vogue* team of hair and makeup people
came to Florida for the shoot in late March, I believe. I got a new
hairstyle and posed by the swimming pool. The interview was about
style and fashion only, so I didn't have to lay my soul bare, which
was a relief. I'm not usually a fan of photo shoots, but this one was
a welcome distraction. It turned out to be a fun day for everyone.

• • •

In early May, my parents went back home to Czechoslovakia and the kids and I returned to New York to finish the school year. I plunged immediately into divorce depositions and got through them thanks to my secret weapon: Ira Garr, my charming but tough attorney. During the hours of depositions, he did the talking while I put on my headphones and cranked Gloria Gaynor's "I Will Survive." The lawyers were going back and forth, and I was singing in my head, "Did you think I'd crumble? Did you think I'd lay down and die?" Well, that was not going to happen. I would survive. (Hey, hey.) That song has probably helped millions of women get through some very rough times. It worked for me.

Don was set to switch to the Hill School, a boarding school in rural Pottstown, Pennsylvania, near the abandoned Bethlehem Steel plant. I'd painstakingly chosen it for him based on the recommendation of a family friend who told me it was a structured but nurturing place. I toured the school a few times and checked out the surrounding area. If Don was going to live away from home at boarding school, it had to be just the right place for him. He'd been excited about gaining some independence and getting out of New York, so I was surprised when he told me that summer that he wasn't sure he wanted to go. He was afraid that if he wasn't around to support me, I would fall apart. It was the sweetest thing I'd ever heard. I assured him that he had his own life to lead and that I'd be okay. In hindsight, though, I think Don may have been right. The kids were my inspiration to stay mentally tough.

I'd had some time to think about what had happened between Donald and me. The very thing that made me a role model for my children and gave me so much personal gratification and pride—my career—probably doomed the marriage. My huge professional wins came at a personal cost. My husband I became more like business partners than spouses. We'd talk about work all the time, about the bottom line, the high rollers coming in that weekend, what was going on at the Plaza. He loved what I did for his company, but, on the other hand, he was frustrated that I spent so much time working.

Behind every successful woman, there is a man in shock. I was *too* successful to be Mrs. Trump. In our marriage, there couldn't be two stars. So one of us had to go.

I resigned in July 1990 from the Trump Organization after a fantastic thirteen-year run. I didn't leave the Plaza high and dry; I stayed for six months so they had time to find my replacement. Most of my handpicked staff left when I did, but I wasn't worried about them. They were well trained with great résumés and I knew they'd land on their feet. The vice president of food and beverage became the manager at the Peninsula. The vice president of operations went to the Pierre.

Immediately after giving notice, I took a six-week vacation to Europe, first taking the kids to my parents' in Czechoslovakia for their annual visit, and then by myself to London for some fashion shows and to reconnect with friends. On that trip, the fog of divorce started to lift. Coming out of hiding was the best medicine for me. My friends supported me and were behind me. I realized that the divorce was truly liberating. I didn't have to answer to a man, at work or at home.

September, as always, felt optimistic. It was the start of a new school year for the kids and a new life for me. It'd been nine months since the Bonnie's incident, and the press in front of Trump Tower had dwindled to just a handful of jackals. I dared to let myself believe that the worst was behind us.

The feeling was short-lived. My children and I were hit out of nowhere with a devastating loss just one month later.

DEATHS IN THE FAMILY

After helping us through the springtime Mar-a-Lago lockdown, my parents returned to their mountain cottage in Moravia where I'd learned to ski and had so many happy memories. The A-frame house sat right on the border between Moravia and Slovakia—in fact, the line ran right through the living room. We joked that it was no-man's-land, a country of our own, and, because it wasn't in one or the other, my parents didn't have to pay taxes!

One evening in October 1990, my father didn't feel well, so Mom and a neighbor took him to the hospital. The doctors said he'd had a heart attack and checked him in. For decades, Dedo had smoked forty cigarettes a day, but he'd quit ten years earlier and, as an unfortunate result, put on a lot of weight. My parents made a plan for Dedo to start exercising and eating better as soon as he was released from the hospital. But he never left. The next day, he had a second heart attack and died at sixty-three. If he'd been in an American hospital, maybe the doctors could have saved him, a thought that would torture me for years to come.

My mother called with the tragic news, and I almost couldn't believe it. I would never see my father again? It didn't seem possible that my first love, my hero, the greatest man I'd ever known, was gone. I told Babi that we would fly to her as soon as possible. My assistant at the time, Lisa Calandra, got on the phone and started dealing with the logistics, calling Don's school, arranging a car to pick him up, organizing our travel plans. I called Donald to tell him what was going on. Pre-split, he and Dedo had always been very close. Donald was shocked and saddened by the news, and immediately offered his private plane to take us to Europe.

I had a little time to compose myself before Ivanka and Eric got home from school and Don arrived by car. They knew something was going on, and Don wanted to know why he'd been pulled out of school. I sat them down and said, "My father passed away this morning. He had a heart attack in the hospital and they couldn't save him."

Their reaction was instantaneous, an explosion of crying and hysterical freaking out. Children's emotions are raw and open. They don't have the layers of defensiveness that adults do. Seeing their pain brought mine to the surface. We hugged and sobbed together.

The next day, we flew to my mother. By the time we landed, she'd already arranged the funeral, which took place three days after the death. As soon as Donald's plane dropped us off, the pilot turned around to go back to New York to get Donald. I was very touched that he brought his mother, Mary, with him for the funeral. She was a kindhearted, generous woman, and it meant a lot to me that she came to pay my father her last respects. (I paid my respects to her at her funeral in 2000, and to Fred Trump the year before hers.) Even though Mary was Scottish and Dedo was Czech, and they came from different worlds and backgrounds, they had a warm relationship. The other mourners were from all eras of my father's life, his friends and colleagues, and our neighbors. Dedo was beloved by so many.

My memories of the funeral in Zlín are blurry at best. I was still in shock. Somehow, the boys put on their suits and Ivanka and I got into our dresses. Dad had an open casket, his body plainly visible, and I was worried that the kids would be afraid or confused. They hadn't experienced loss yet or seen a dead body. Eric was too small, only six, and didn't ask any questions. Ivanka and Don understood that although Dedo's body was in the coffin, his essence and spirit were not there anymore.

Pallbearers carried the casket into the cemetery in the woods nearby, and we said our prayers and threw flowers on the casket as it was lowered into the ground. I remember my kids' faces, crushed with suffering. I did my best to comfort them, but there was little I could say that would ease the pain of losing someone they were all so close to. Don had spent summers at the chalet, just him and Dedo, for years. At that time, he was only barely speaking to Donald. Looking back, I can hardly believe what Don went through in that one calendar year: the split, the media onslaught and public divorce, moving away from home to boarding school, and then the passing of his beloved grandfather. All the while, he was constantly aware and concerned about how his siblings and I were coping.

Throughout that horrible day, he kept one eye on Ivanka and Eric. Don's strength at twelve amazes me to this day.

The boys would like to say a few words about Dedo:

─────────────────── ERIC ───────────────────

Dedo was a huge influence in our life. In Florida and Greenwich, we spent countless hours fishing with him. He bought me my first BB guns and a 50cc Suzuki dirt bike, which Don and I treasured. Dedo was an engineer, and he loved working with his hands. If he could design it, he could build it.

─────────────────── DON ───────────────────

Every summer while growing up, I'd go to Czechoslovakia by myself and spend five or six weeks with my grandfather. My grandparents didn't speak English very well at the time, so I had no choice but to learn to speak Czech fluently from a very young age. By going there, I understood how lucky we were in the US, to have what we had and to grow up the way we were growing up. But I also saw the potential pitfalls of privilege. My parents and grandparents wanted me to see another side of life, where relationships and spending good times together were most important. It was an incredibly valuable lesson that really helped me learn how not to take superficial things in life too seriously, and not to take intangible things for granted.

Apart from the joy and happiness that my wife and

family bring me today, I can honestly say that being in Czechoslovakia with my grandfather was the most memorable time in my life. My grandpa would say, "There's the woods. See you at dark!" He taught me to fish, rock-climb, camp, shoot with a bow and an air rifle. Czechoslovakian summers were my introduction to "the great outdoors" and an era that lives in me that I hand down to my children. I was blessed to have such a wonderful person in my life. I miss him. I will always miss him.

The funeral and burial took place on Ivanka's ninth birthday. Needless to say, she didn't have a party that year.

For days afterward, photos of my family at the burial popped up in international newspapers. Paparazzi were hiding behind every tree at the cemetery. My father wasn't a celebrity. He was a humble, dignified man and his farewell was supposed to be private and intimate, for close friends and family only. It was yet another violation of our anguish by the media. I was distraught on behalf of my children, who wanted to cry and grieve in peace, and my mother, who was saying good-bye to her love of forty-five years. My father's death was so sudden, I didn't have time to tell any of my New York friends about it. I just got on the plane, leaving no word of where I was going. Back in the city, Fashion Week was under way, and my absence was noticed by the press and designers, especially at the dozen shows at the Plaza Hotel (this was before the Bryant Park and Lincoln Center–centric Fashion Weeks). "Where's Ivana?" asked the fashion press. The paparazzi photos of my entire family in black, weeping at the grave site, gave them their answer.

We flew home a week later to a life of loss. I handled the death and grieving process with the kids by being frank and forward thinking. Don and Ivanka looked to me for cues about how to grieve. I told them that we should mourn and be sad but accept the reality of death. "When it's your time, it's your time," I said. It's my style not to wallow in the unfairness of untimely death but to feel blessed to be alive. When Jiří died, my pain spurred my escape to the West. When I lost my father, I was reminded of the brevity of life and was inspired to get on with mine, and to make it fabulous for myself and my children. If I had any lingering doubts about ending my marriage, I buried them at my father's funeral.

The one saving grace of the timing of my father's death was that he lived long enough to see the fall of communism in Czechoslovakia: by his death, student-led demonstrations in Prague had driven out the Soviet-controlled government. On November 24, 1989, the communist leadership resigned en masse, and a parliamentary republic took shape. Since the transfer of power was peaceful, with not a single shot fired, it was called the Velvet Revolution. After forty-one years of oppression, Czechoslovakia—now the Czech Republic—was free.

A year after that, in March 1992, my divorce became final, and I was free as well.

It'd been a rough couple of years for the children. They'd been through more in their young lives than many adults will ever face in theirs. But hard times weren't over for them yet. They would have to withstand another tragedy, one very close to home.

The Friday night of Memorial Day weekend 1993, I was in

Tampa at the Home Shopping Network, doing my show. The kids were in Greenwich with Bridget, and the plan was for me to fly up in the morning. Don was home for the long weekend, and I couldn't wait to see him. We were all excited about being together again.

While filming the show, I'd chat with another host about the products for an hour or so, then the camera would zoom in on her for a few minutes while she talked about the ingredients in the face cream or the fabric in a blouse, giving me a chance to take a quick bathroom break or have a sip of water. On that night, during a break, I quickly called Greenwich, but, weirdly, no one answered. I assumed Bridget had taken the kids out to dinner or they were playing outdoors. Patrick the houseman had already gone home for the night to his family.

Ivanka had gone to bed, but Bridget hadn't tucked her in yet, which struck Ivanka as strange. Even at thirteen, Ivanka liked it when Bridget came to wish her good night and say a quick prayer before sleep. It was how she sealed the day, and when Bridget didn't come in, Ivanka got worried. She got out of bed, found Eric and Don watching TV in the living room, and asked them if they'd seen Bridget. The boys volunteered to go looking for her and to send her to Ivanka. She went back to bed, and the boys searched the house.

ERIC

We were at the Greenwich house and the phone started ringing and ringing. It was around eight p.m. Bridget didn't want any of us picking up the phone because we were young kids, so she always answered it. But it just kept ringing. After Ivanka asked if we'd seen her, Don and I went downstairs to find her. Bridget was in the basement, unconscious. I was pretty young, but I knew looking at her that it wasn't good.

I got off the air finally, and the producers told me that I'd had a few urgent messages from my children. My heart leapt into my throat, and I called them back. Don told me, "Bridget passed out. The ambulance came to take her to the hospital." He'd also called Patrick, who was there now with the kids. He said the situation was under control, but I could hear in Don's voice that he was rattled, upset.

I caught my flight and was back home as soon as possible. By the time I landed, Bridget had died of a heart attack, the same thing that killed my father. She was sixty-seven. I told Don how proud I was of him for handling a horrific situation and for being brave and strong for his little sister and brother. Eric was only ten. That weekend was the first time he'd been with his brother in months. Eric stuck to Don like glue.

Ivanka was inconsolable. There was nothing I could say that would bring Bridget back or take away her pain, so I just held her and let her cry in my arms. Over the next few days, I assured her that Bridget had had a good life. She'd devoted herself to caring for children, first with the Kennedy family and then with ours. Bridget never liked me much—she always took two steps back when I entered a room—but she adored the kids, especially Ivanka, and took great satisfaction in running the household with precision and detail. She had nervous hands. I can still picture her walking in the kitchen, wringing those hands: the picture of a woman who had things to take care of.

In time, I gave Ivanka the only advice I could, saying, "What's done is done. You have to accept it, roll with the ups and downs, and get on with your life." It might sound unsentimental to some, but falling apart was not an option. You had to dry your tears and go on. The living owe that much to the departed. We had a small service for Bridget's friends and our family in New York. Donald arranged for her body to be flown to her family in Ireland, where she was laid to rest.

I continued to live in Trump Tower until 1994, when I found a town house on East Sixty-Fourth Street. It needed a lot of work. No one had lived there in twelve years, and its last incarnation had been as a dentist's office with lots of small rooms. I hired George Gregorian, a designer I'd worked with at the Plaza who knew my taste well, and we got to work. I opened my Filofax full of contractors and designers I'd worked with in the past and made some calls. They ran a bulldozer through the lobby to gut everything. A job that would ordinarily take five years was finished in one.

I could go on for page after page about the renovations—putting in the staircase, molding, and chandeliers—but suffice it to say, my home reflects my style perfectly. Here's the briefest description:

The parlor floor includes the entryway, a powder room, and Dorothy's and the in-house lawyer's offices.

On the second floor, up the marble staircase or the birdcage elevator, are my French-inspired living room, the white piano room, the dining room with a crystal chandelier, and a galley kitchen (I don't cook much anymore), with floor-to-ceiling views of my terrace and garden out back.

The third floor is my floor: the leopard sitting room; the master bedroom, with a gold-embossed fireplace and Chinese murals that I had restored by artists referred to me by the Metropolitan Museum of Art; and a pink-marble bathroom.

On the fourth floor is what used to be Ivanka's room, now a guest room, with a fireplace, a canopy bed, a large bathroom, and a huge closet, as well as Eric's old room with a bathroom, and my mother's room.

The fifth floor has two maids' rooms and my closet, which goes on, and on, and on. I call it Indochine, because by the time you get to the end of it, you might as well be in another continent.

The top floor has a huge gym that used to be Don's bedroom, a bathroom, and two maids' rooms. Donatella Versace used to be my across-the-street neighbor. My home gym was on the same level as her dressing room. We used to wave at each other while I was on the treadmill and she was getting ready for her day.

I've lived here for twenty-three years and guided my kids through their teenage years here. I've lived and loved here. I could make a hefty profit if I sold it, but I'm never leaving this house. They'll have to carry me out in a box first.

- 18 -

20/20 HINDSIGHT

In 1991, while Donald and I were still in the throes of negotiating our settlement, I appeared on my friend Barbara Walters's newsmagazine show *20/20* and talked about the split and its aftermath. Barbara asked me about the day in Aspen when the showgirl accosted me, and other subjects that were still tender. After a full year of keeping a stiff upper lip, not talking to the press about the split, and never showing my private agony to anyone, Barbara Walters made me cry! On national television!

Some friend *she* is. (I'm joking, of course. I adore and respect her and have valued her friendship for forty years.)

Twenty-six years later, I have perfect 20/20 hindsight about that chaotic time in our lives. My conscience is clear. I was a loyal wife during my marriage to Donald and a great mother during a singularly agonizing time. I'm not angry with Donald anymore. Once our legal battle was over, we settled into our roles as companionable coparents. Basically, I told him what I was going to do, and he agreed with me. The final result of our joint effort turned out pretty well. We raised three magnificent kids, despite what they went through in the early nineties.

They are all at peace with the divorce, too. Ivanka often says that she learned to be optimistic during that horrible time, which was the attitude I relentlessly reinforced by saying, "It's going to be fine," over and over again. The media onslaught forced us to close ranks and isolate ourselves. Eric credits that bunker mentality for cementing the sibling bond. Before the split, they got along well. But after, they were a united front, protecting and supporting each other against anyone who'd think to do them harm. Ivanka says that she grew closer to her father after he moved out of the triplex. She visited him more often and called him frequently from school. He always took her calls, no matter what. He often interrupted meetings and put her on speakerphone to say hello to everyone there.

Don eventually forgave his father. The strategy to remove him from the tension physically and emotionally by sending him to boarding school worked. He was thirteen when he left home, which seems very young in hindsight. But it turned out to be the right decision.

DON

During my five years at the Hill School, a lot of doors opened for me, and I did a lot of growing up.

Moving to rural Pennsylvania also got me out of the city. Even though I was born in New York, it was never my thing. I didn't like the congestion and the noise. I always wanted to be outside. Still do. Every weekend for the last decade, our family has left New York on Friday afternoon for the country. I'm out of my suit and into Carhartts. We don't come back until late Sunday night. Spending as much time outdoors as possible is our family's lifestyle. I appreciate what the city has to offer for my kids, but I also would like to show them another life roaming in the woods on the weekends. Hunting and fishing kept me out of trouble growing up, and I want my kids to have that same opportunity. If you have to wake up at five a.m. to get to the tree stand, you can't stay up partying.

As part of the settlement, I had Mar-a-Lago rights for one month each year, but it was too weird to go there. I loved Palm Beach, though, so I bought my own house, called Concha Marina, a gorgeous place designed by Addison Mizner, a famous architect who designed Worth Avenue, the shopping street in town. He actually built Concha Marina for himself in 1924 in the Spanish Moorish style with roof tiles from Cuba. It has a tunnel going from my house, under South Ocean Boulevard, to a private beach. Only four houses in Palm Beach have tunnels like this: mine, Mar-a-Lago, the Kennedy compound, and one other. It isn't fun after a hurricane, when the tunnel fills with sand and it takes two weeks to dig it out. But on nice days, it's a good way to get to the beach.

The kids and I snorkeled at the coral reef near the jetty at the end of the property and came upon a huge barracuda, as big as a couch. I remember hearing once that as long as you don't turn your back on barracudas, they won't attack you, so we'd make eye contact with him every few seconds. When we swam back to shore, we went backward. At the time, I thought, *I lost a husband and gained a gigantic barracuda*. It seemed like a good deal.

(Epilogue on the barracuda: He was the Concha Marina mascot for nine years, and then one day, we went down at the start of the season, and he was gone. It felt like the end of an era.)

After the showgirl got pregnant and had a daughter, Donald married her. The whole world was watching. He couldn't *not* wed the mother of his new baby, regardless of whether his heart was really in it. None of the children went to Donald's Christmas 1993 wedding, and not because I asked them to protest it. It wasn't my business. We didn't speak at home about it at all. They issued a statement to the press, saying, "In discussions among ourselves, we decided to stay in Aspen with our mother and grandmother." I appreciated my children's company and support.

As for their half sister, Tiffany (Donald got to give that name to a daughter after all), my children are all close with her. When Tiffany was born, I asked Ivanka, then twelve, how she felt about having a new half sister. She said, "This child didn't do anything wrong to anybody and I'm not going to be mean or nasty to her." She immediately assumed the role of protective big sister to Tiffany, which she still is today.

Two years ago, I was at Mar-a-Lago with the whole family for Eric's wedding to Lara. We posed for a family picture after the ceremony. I was standing next to Donald and on his other side was a young woman. I whispered to Donald, "Who's that?"

He said, "Tiffany."

I was shocked. The last time I'd seen her, she was a little girl. And now she's a lovely young woman, and a graduate of Donald, Ivanka, and Don's alma mater, the University of Pennsylvania. She is a law student and will likely join the Trump Organization to work alongside her half brothers. I wish her well.

Her mother, on the other hand . . .

I'm not saying that if it weren't for the showgirl, Donald and I would still be together or that my life since our divorce hasn't been a wonderful adventure full of love, travel, success, and laughter. I've had a fabulous life. But that woman knowingly entered into a relationship with my husband, the father of three small children. She actively participated in humiliating me in the media and indirectly put my kids at risk *for months*. I went through hell, and then I was expected to be okay with her being around my children? We all have deep scars from that period of our lives, in part due to her actions. The fact that the kids and I came through the entire ordeal stronger is irrelevant.

Recently, she tried to bury the hatchet with me via the *Daily Mail* in London. They called to ask if I accepted the apology and I said, "Apology *not* accepted." This woman broke up my marriage and took away my kids' father. I don't care how sorry she is. She told *People* magazine last year, "If [Ivana is] holding any kind of resentment toward me, I really hope, for her sake, that she can forgive me." For *my* sake? She wants my absolution for *her* sake! I'm doing just fine with my resentment, thank you very much. *People* interviewed her because she went on *Dancing with the Stars*. What a disgrace that was. No class! I've been asked to be a contestant on the show a hundred times—and offered a mint—but I wouldn't go on that show, dancing in those tiny dresses with the boobs and butt hanging out.

I'm not opposed to reality TV in general. I've appeared on a couple of reality shows and had a lot of fun doing them. But my exploits in the genre aired years ago, long before my ex was running for the highest office in the land. The showgirl appeared on *DWTS* when (because) her ex-husband was running for president! It was disrespectful to do the show. I never would have embarrassed Donald that way.

The day of Donald's inauguration in January 2017, I was invited to sit in the front row on the main platform with my ninety-two-year-old mother. She can walk and climb stairs, but not very fast. With all the people, cars and buses, and equipment everywhere, I thought it'd be easier to put her in a wheelchair to get her around, but that didn't work out. I couldn't maneuver the chair through the narrow aisles of the front rows, plus it was freezing cold and crowded, a logistical nightmare. So I made the decision to watch from a spot off the platform where we could make a fast getaway. As soon as it was over, we got out of there and went straight to the airport. I wanted to get my mother safely back to New York.

I woke up the next day to headlines that claimed I fled the inauguration to avoid an awkward run-in with Marla freaking Maples at the party that night. I didn't even know she was there! It was ridiculous. I'd been invited to the inaugural parties, but after the horrible afternoon, I wasn't in the mood. The prospect of standing around a Washington, DC, ballroom and schmoozing politicians held zero appeal. I would have liked to see my children, but getting my mother home was more important.

That said, I'm glad I didn't see Marla that day, or any other day since our two-minute confrontation in 1989 in Aspen.

Melania Trump: I have no problems with her at all. Why should I? She didn't break up my marriage. Her son, Barron, eleven, plays often with my grandchildren. Donald is happy with her and our interactions have been cordial. We hit a minor speed bump in the fall of 2015, when Donald was on the road to the White House. I was having lunch for forty female friends in New York and I asked, "Who is voting for Donald?" That started a conversation about what a Trump presidency would be like, and all I said was that Melania is a quiet, private woman, and that she might not enjoy being in public so much. The next thing I knew, the *Daily News* was running an article quoting an "insider" who claimed I said, "[Melania] can't talk, she can't give a speech, she doesn't go to events, she doesn't seem to want to be involved."

Ivanka called me that day and said Melania was upset about the article. I hadn't even heard about it yet, and told my daughter I didn't say those things and that the paper never called to ask me to comment. I texted Melania, saying, "You have never done anything wrong to me and I never have to you. You are in the family and I would never do anything against the family. Love, Ivana." That smoothed things over. I hope she knows I'm rooting for her, just as I'm rooting for Donald. I believe he'll be a great president and that she'll surprise a lot of people and be a wonderful First Lady. She surprised me already when she announced she was taking over

Michelle Obama's organic garden. Somehow, I can't picture her in jeans and work gloves, holding a shovel.

Frankly, I wouldn't want to be in Melania's Louboutins right now. Back in the eighties, Ronald Reagan sent Donald a letter asking him to run for president, and I thought it was a great idea. But then the scandal happened and the press hated him, so a run was out. I believe in always looking to the future and never asking, "What if?" But in this one case, if the affair had never happened and Donald had run in '92 and won, I'd have whipped the White House staff into shape in ten days.

On the other hand, I would hate to be in the world of politics. The nature of it seems to be all talking and lying, making false promises, and then nothing gets done. Donald is trying to change that, but I'm not interested in bashing my head into a brick wall. Growing up, I distrusted and feared politicians and the police. No, I don't want anything to do with Washington, which is a crooked, boring city. What do people do for fun at the White House? Throw bowling balls in the basement with security guards watching your every move. Forget it. I'd rather have my freedom and be a secret adviser to Donald from the comfort of my town house, should he call.

PART FIVE

PRIDE OF
THE LION MOM

THE VALUE OF A DOLLAR

I am a bottom-line person. The bottom line about cash and kids? When they're very young, you have to teach them that money doesn't fall off trees or they'll turn into rotten, entitled brats. Although my children certainly went on lavish vacations and had more objects than the average family, compared to others at our income level, they had significantly less.

I lived well and enjoyed my luxuries, but the kids understood that I'd earned them through hard work. What I shared with them didn't belong to them. I have heard rich kids—like the ones in Jamie Johnson's documentary *Born Rich*, which Ivanka appeared in—talk about their parents' houses and cars as if they were the kids' own possessions. My children never had such a foolish misconception. My Ferrari was mine. My yacht was mine. I even named it

M.Y. Ivana. Of course, they could and did cruise with me whenever they liked, but they didn't have a sense of ownership of it. (No one, not even my precious children, was allowed to put one big toe in the Ferrari.)

Back in the nineties and aughts, when Don, Ivanka, and Eric were growing up, the scions of the superrich and famous were tracked by Page Six and *Vanity Fair* on their jaunts to Ibiza, nightclub benders in Las Vegas, shopping sprees on Rodeo Drive, tantrums in first class. They embarrassed their families and disgraced themselves in drunken, drugged-out, compromising situations. What made the mortification possible? Their parents' open wallets and platinum credit cards.

What idiot would give a high school kid a monthly allowance of $10,000 and expect that to go well? Kim Kardashian's father gave her a Mercedes for her Sweet Sixteen. Did he think that would keep her close to home and out of trouble? A pair of famous sisters around Ivanka's age apparently had an unlimited clothing budget, flew in a private jet wherever and whenever they liked, and were mainstays at Studio 54 and Limelight in tenth grade. I wonder if they even went to class, took a test, or picked up a book, ever.

When my kids were at school, I gave them a modest allowance for everything besides tuition and housing: clothes, food, school supplies, fun. They didn't need more than what I gave them and could have survived on far less. If they wanted to take a friend for pizza or a burger, they could afford it, but it wasn't nearly enough to hop on an airplane and party in a suite at the Bellagio.

The idea of giving a teenager his or her own credit card was absurd to me. Don, Ivanka, and Eric were never handed Visas or Amexes by me. When they were in New York and needed to go shopping for essentials, I would give them the cash I deemed appropriate.

"What about in case of an emergency?" Ivanka once asked when she wanted a card of her own.

"In case of an emergency, call me," I replied.

When Don went to boarding school in Pennsylvania, I wanted to make sure he called his grandmother and me regularly to check in, so I gave him a phone card. It worked out well for a year or two. And then one day, the bill arrived and it was four times the usual amount. I knew he hadn't talked to me for hundreds of minutes that month. It turned out, fifteen-year-old Don had been burning up the phone lines talking to a girl. I was happy he had a special friend (shocked, but glad). However, I wasn't going to finance his long-distance romance. "If you want to call me or your grandmother, I'll pay for it," I said. "But if you want to chat with your girlfriend, do it on your own dime."

Occasionally, the kids lobbied me for cash to buy medium-ticket items, like a new handbag or pair of skis. The rule was that they had to convince me that the expense was absolutely necessary. If Eric asked for a new bike, I'd ask, "What's wrong with the old one?" If he made a legitimate case that his old bike was terrible and that he could not function until he got a new one, I'd praise his negotiating skills and say, "Okay, sweetie. You can have a new bike . . . at Christmas."

If Eric then asked his father, "Daddy, can I have a new bike?" Donald would ask, "What did your mother say? If she said no, she had a reason."

Donald and I agreed that kids and cash don't mix. But, as we told them, if they earned the money themselves, they had every right to spend it however they wanted—as long as it wasn't on drugs, alcohol, or cigarettes. The kids begged me for odd jobs to earn some extra cash. Don cut grass with a lawn mower in Greenwich for an entire summer to buy himself a new fly-fishing rod, even though the old one was just as good. In the long run, he might've wished he'd saved that money for something else. If they were old enough to make their own money, they were free to make their own mistakes about spending it. They learned as teenagers how to make long-term, smart purchasing decisions.

ERIC

One of the reasons I started working at twelve on construction sites was to earn money to buy things for myself. Others kids from wealthy families, people we knew, were given unlimited funds, ridiculous allowances, and cars. They would go out, spend a fortune, and get in trouble. The thought of me busting my chops breaking down walls, doing the toughest kind of manual labor at construction sites for minimum wage with a great team of men, and then going out at the end of the week and blowing my paycheck on booze or drugs? That is not how I was raised. You never saw Don, Ivanka, or me really getting into trouble. To this day, we are always the first people in the office in the morning and the last people to leave. We were conditioned to connect hard work with self-respect and a feeling of accomplishment. It's where our drive comes from.

Whenever I took the kids to Saint-Tropez or St. Moritz for vacations, they flew economy while I was in first class. I'd say, "Have a good flight. I'll see you when we land." They were small and could curl up in the seats and sleep. They'd wake up in France or Switzerland and have croissants. What did they have to complain about? Ivanka once tried to talk me into giving her an upgrade. I heard her out and then said, "As soon as you can pay for the upgrade yourself, you can have it." During Donald's presidential campaign, Ivanka was flying JetBlue with her kids to Florida, and, while boarding, an angry passenger started yelling at her about her father and the election. Ivanka was as polite and composed as ever in that awkward situation. The media praised her poise and unflappability, but some wondered why she was flying JetBlue in coach instead of in a private plane or in first class. I laughed out loud. Ivanka *always* flew economy!

As for the kids' clothing budgets, it was minimal, because they wore school uniforms on weekdays. Otherwise, the boys couldn't have cared less about fashion. Don would be thrilled to wear jeans and a flannel every day. Ivanka does have an eye for nice things. If she wanted something cool and new, I took her shopping with me with a clear agenda and a concise list in mind. Spoiled kids view spending money as a form of entertainment, a cure for boredom. I taught mine that shopping is like running an errand, a necessary evil to endure once or twice a year. We made a back-to-school September shopping trip to Bloomingdale's for casual and sporting clothes, a few cocktail dresses for Ivanka, and blazers, trousers, and shirts for the boys. We'd go again during their spring breaks for T-shirts, shorts, and bathing suits.

People think I have a black belt in shopping, but I actually can't stand it. I have a system that makes it as painless and fast as possible. Every year, I spend half a day at Bloomie's to pick up face cream and lingerie. If I like something, I buy a dozen sets in beige, a dozen in white, and a dozen in black. I send three of each color to Saint-Tropez, Miami, and New York. For suits and dresses, I can always shop in my closet! I still go to a few Fashion Week shows a year—including Dennis Basso, Carolina Herrera, Roberto Cavalli, Zang Toi, Domenico Vacca, and Marc Bouwer—with an eye toward comfortable, easy dresses, but I'm not the fashion maven I once was. I'm actually selling a lot of my vintage couture, in case anyone's interested, and donating dozens upon dozens to charity.

Ivanka's solution to not having a big clothing budget of her own when she was a teenager? She went shopping in my Indochine closet, choosing among the racks for blouses and skirts, dresses and suits. She still does. Two years ago, she was going to an eighties-themed party and called Dorothy (I was in France) to ask if she could come over to my town house and rummage in my closet for a Bob Mackie gold-, silver-, and white-striped beaded flapper dress. She found it and wore it to the party. The next day, the papers ran a picture of her in the dress alongside an old photo of me in the frock in all-white. Ivanka knows she can raid my closet whenever she wants, as long as she brings everything back (I'm still waiting for a red Dior dress to be returned . . .). She can borrow my jewelry, too. Over the years, I've seen photos of her in the papers and said, "So *that's* where my diamond necklace ran off to." It warms my heart that we share clothes. When she was a little girl, she played dress-up in my things, always going right for the high heels and clomping around in them. Those days are over, though. Her feet are one size bigger than mine so she can't raid my shoe collection anymore. It's kind of a shame. I don't wear my heels often. The only shoes I wear these days are Ivanka Trump ballet flats! Maybe Ivanka's daughter, Arabella, can pick up where her mom left off and take some stilettos off my hands.

HOW TO TALK TO ANYONE

Last year, Eric was on a flight to Scotland, and a comedian named Mohammed Amer sat down in the seat next to him. Apparently, the woman seated behind Eric warned Amer not to go anywhere near my son, assuming (wrongly) that Eric was prejudiced against Muslims. But Amer sat down anyway, and immediately launched into a conversation with Eric about immigration and discrimination. Amer told the Huffington Post afterward, "I just know we had a good, decent conversation, and I think that proves that we can talk to each other, and I think that's what's most important." He posted a smiling photo of the two of them on his Facebook page.

Breaking news! My smart, friendly son can have a pleasant conversation with a stranger on an airplane! Stop the freaking presses.

My children were raised to have manners and be polite, and to engage in conversation. In a real way, Don, Ivanka, and Eric talk for a living. Right now, the boys are in the business world and have interactions with a wide range of people every hour of the day. The first call of the day might be with a billionaire banker. The next might be with a plumber. Ivanka is in politics now, which requires next-level conversation skills. In a single day, Ivanka might do an on-camera press interview, go to a parent-teacher conference, attend an inner-circle meeting in the Oval Office, and sit next to world leaders like Justin Trudeau or Angela Merkel in the Cabinet Room.

One of the greatest gifts I've ever given to my children is the gift of gab. I trained them to hold their own in conversation with *anyone, anywhere*, at a construction site or a black-tie event. It doesn't matter whom you're speaking to, as long as you're polite, respectful, confident, and articulate, with good eye contact and a friendly smile.

GIRL TALK

I didn't spoil my kids, but I loved to indulge my friends. Every December, I hosted a decadent holiday luncheon at Trump Tower for eight or so of my closest pals. Every summer, I took a few dozen of them on the *Trump Princess*—a three-hundred-foot yacht—on a cruise of the Jersey coast. Every September, I invited six friends to lunch at our box at the US Open to see the quarterfinals matches. But my favorite friend gathering was the annual girlfriend weekend every spring at Mar-a-Lago. I'd invite twenty of my best pals for three days of excellent food, spa treatments, tennis, snorkeling, and ladies-only relaxation under the Florida sun, and Ivanka was with us the entire time, just another one of the girls.

Before everyone arrived, I'd ask each guest what she'd like to do while she was in Palm Beach, write down the requests, and make a personalized schedule for each woman for all three days packed with exercise classes in the dance pavilion where Marjorie Merriweather Post, the original owner of the property, used to have square dances; massages; naps; facials; golf lessons—anything her heart desired. If all twenty of them wanted a predinner massage at the same time, twenty massage therapists would be there with warm oils ready to go. On Friday, I flew the group down on a private plane, and the weekend began. The days were casual, but every evening, we put on fancy dresses for a moonlight dinner on the beach, with plentiful margaritas and strolling mariachis. One year, my friend Cathie Koos showed up at dinner in a Donald Duck costume. We all died.

The tradition ended after the divorce, but we had a ton of fun while it lasted. I made sure of it. One weekend, I went to the kitchen to see about the lunch and came back to the pool to find it deserted. I asked one of the butlers, "Where is everyone?"

"They went to the beach," he replied.

I walked through the private tunnel to the beach and found them all ... topless! I screamed, "Girls! Put on your tops! We're right next to the snobs at the Bath & Tennis Club. They can see you! I'll be run out of town!" Sure enough, some of the members, the old men with the red noses, were gawking at the fence. The girls put their tops back on. I was not run out of town.

That was as close as any men got to Mar-a-Lago during the

girlfriend weekends, although one did try to schmooze his way in. Sylvester Stallone was with Brigitte Nielsen in Miami and called Donald to say he would like to visit Mar-a-Lago that weekend. Donald told him I was having a private party and no men were allowed, not even him. But Stallone didn't take no for an answer. He called me directly and said, "Hi, Ivana. It's Sly. I'd like to come see you tomorrow."

I said, "I'm sorry, but no men are allowed!"

"But I have such a great body, Ivana. Your friends will love to have me."

"You know what? So do I!" I said, and hung up. He came the following weekend. His body was definitely worth the wait—and so was Brigitte's.

——————————— IVANKA ———————————

I remember my mother's women's retreat weekends at Mar-a-Lago. Part of the weekend was an acrobics class with all of her girlfriends, and they wore these amazing, vivid-colored outfits that were pure Jane Fonda, skin-tight, with color-coordinated headbands and leg warmers. I didn't join in the class, but I remember watching them from the side, mesmerized by the parade of colors.

Mom used to put me to work whenever she had a party. It started when I would just do some drawings for fun, and she loved them so much she would give me the assignment of making twenty or thirty drawings to use as place mats for a lunch, and personalizing them for each guest. I would make a production assembly line with construction paper and crayons to get it done in time.

Once, I made these paperweights for all her friends. I'd pour Lucite on top of carefully selected flowers and seashells in a mold, and then I'd use tweezers to insert little slips of paper with each woman's name, handwritten, into the plastic before it hardened.

I was the entertainment, too. There was a theater at Mar-a-Lago. After dinner, my mother and her friends would go have drinks there, and I'd get on the stage and perform for them. I loved the show *Annie* and sang "Tomorrow." I went through a Madonna phase and would do all her hits—"Vogue" definitely, and "Express Yourself"—with dancing. Mom's friends would watch and give me a round of applause. I remember being really excited about doing it, too.

SMALL TALK

I regularly hosted parties at Trump Tower. When the guests started to arrive, I sent the kids to the living room to entertain them. I would come down in fifteen minutes, fashionably late, and then relieve the kids of their host duties. "This is what you're going to do," I instructed. "Go downstairs, say, 'Hello, I'm Don' or 'Eric' or 'Ivanka.' Take a drink order. Speak to everyone as they come in. No sitting on the sofa by yourself! Stay on your feet and go from person to person. A little small talk, a little *coochi coochi, moochi moochi.* 'How are you?' 'How is the weather?' 'How do you know my parents?' 'I just came from ballet' or 'soccer' or 'karate.'"

Sometimes, I would spy on the kids before I made my entrance.

"Hello, I'm Don Trump. Can I take your coat?"

"Hi, I'm Ivanka Trump. Mom is on her way down. How are you?"

Fabio, a male model for countless romance novel covers, came to one of my parties, and Ivanka's composure was shaken. She blushed adorably when they shook hands. He was, and still is, a very handsome man! I believe she got him a drink and moved on to the next guest without being too flustered.

When I made my entrance, guests would say, "Your children are so polite! What great manners!" They seemed so surprised, as if they'd never met children who looked them in the eye before. It was disarming to see a nine-year-old working the room, mingling with movie stars, politicians, and financiers with grace and confidence. They weren't forced to do it, but it was expected. Entertaining was just a part of being in our family. The kids were never afraid of talking to adults or self-conscious about going up to strangers and introducing themselves, because they did it often from a young age. It's a bit like skiing. The younger you start, the less fear you have, and the better you are at it.

One day in the late eighties, I was by the pool with the major-domo of Mar-a-Lago, and we got a phone call from the Royal Air Force, from Prince Charles's social secretary. That night, Charles was the guest of honor at a gala hosted by upper-crusty horsey people at the International Polo Club in Wellington, Florida. His social secretary said that the plane was landing at the West Palm Beach airport in one hour and, if it wouldn't be too much trouble, might Prince Charles pop by for a tour of Mar-a-Lago?

In other words, I had sixty minutes to organize a royal reception!

As soon as I hung up, my assistant and I got on the phones and called thirty of my friends. "Get over here, now," I said. "And dress modestly!" Estée Lauder showed up fifteen minutes later looking like Queen Elizabeth in a hat, pearls, a conservative dress, gloves, and a boxy clutch. Charles's security team arrived before he did to go over the property and the grounds, checking under every bush with bomb-sniffing dogs. They asked me for a list of every person who would be at the tea, including the family, our friends, and the staff. I had to scramble to get a list of eighty names together in ten minutes.

And then he arrived via limo. Prince Charles was charming, gracious, and friendly. He was very interested in the history of the house and asked a lot of questions during the tour. Afterward, he posed for pictures with everyone. Our adult guests, who were usually the opposite of shrinking violets, were a bit shy to meet him. But the kids were as cool as the cucumbers in the tiny sandwiches. Don, Ivanka, and Eric walked right up to him, introduced themselves, shook his hand, and asked, "How are you?" "How was your flight?" "Can I get you a drink?" (Charles skipped the tea and had whiskey instead.)

SOUND BITES

Oprah. Barbara Walters. Jay Leno. The kids faced off with all of them. Although they grew up watching their parents talk to the press, I can't say that either one of us gave the kids concrete instructions on dealing with the media. It's a natural instinct, an innate intelligence. You either have it or you don't.

If they were paying attention, the kids got the best media training money could buy from Donald and me. We were always in front of the camera or headlining events with prepared speeches or off-the-cuff remarks. Trained public speakers can go for an hour without notes and then do fifteen minutes of Q & A. I used to do it all the time on the lecture circuit. The kids attended enough of them to learn how it's done. There's nothing to be afraid of if you are expressing yourself freely and honestly.

Once, when Ivanka was just starting out in the Trump Organization, Donald brought her along to a meeting so she could watch him in action. But then, completely spontaneously, he called her up onstage to address the crowd for him. It was a sink-or-swim situation for her, not unlike the time my father took me out to the middle of the lake and said, "Now swim back to shore." Ivanka was nervous at first, but once she started talking, she realized she knew her stuff and did very well. As I said before, you either have it or you don't.

Before a speaking engagement or media appearance, I make sure I think ahead and plan answers to predictable questions, including the ones I'd rather not have to deal with at all. I can tell what kind of response reporters want by their tone of voice and the way they look at me. If the tone is hostile, I ignore the question or I'll say, "Well . . ." and then stop talking. The reporter is forced to wait for me to say something, and when I don't, they have dead air, which is the worst thing for TV. The reporter has to move on to the next question.

Eric and Ivanka really enjoyed their multiple seasons on *The Apprentice* and *The Celebrity Apprentice*. The shooting schedule was tough on them and they were often too busy to meet me for lunch, which was my only complaint about their TV stardom. I watched the show to see them on it, but I didn't find it suspenseful in the least. I could always predict which person would get fired because I know how Donald thinks.

Needless to say, all three kids were magnificent at the Republican National Convention, giving articulate, impassioned speeches to support their father. Don presented with real confidence and authority, but I don't think he enjoys the spotlight, or how the media can spin the most innocent comment into something offensive. No matter how articulate you might be, CNN or the *New York Times* will use your words to reinforce their own agenda. This is why I didn't get involved with the press at that time. "Too many cooks in the kitchen," I said. Don was a good sport this winter when the *Times* ran an article with a strange and stiff photo of him sitting on a tree stump. The Internet turned it into a meme making fun of his rigid posture. He could have been upset, but he started posting the images on Instagram to show people that he thought some of them were funny, too. You learn not to take things personally.

Eric is very good at controlling interviews. If he doesn't like a question, he ignores it and talks about what he wants to discuss, always smiling. It's beautiful to watch.

Ivanka holds the reins tightly. Even though she's the most publicly visible of my children, she rarely gives interviews these days and prefers to control her image carefully through her own social media. When a public dust storm whips up, she waits for it to pass without comment. To me, that's Ivanka being smart. She knows that when you throw gasoline on a fire, it only gets bigger. But if you cut off the oxygen, it dies down. She has to be especially careful now in her role as assistant to the president. As she told Gayle King on *CBS This Morning*, the most important conversations she'll have with her father will probably never be revealed in public. Sometimes, the most impactful words anyone can say are softly spoken, delivered at precisely the right moment in the right ear.

KIDS WHO WORK

In order to be liked by their kids, many parents do everything for them. I didn't really care how popular I was at home and made it clear that the children had to carry their own weight. They made their own beds and kept their own rooms neat. On the slopes, they hauled their own equipment. Granted, the nannies or housekeepers might have remade the bed and reorganized the toys, but the kids gave it their finest effort.

"If you make a mess," I said, "you clean it up."

"Why do I have to?"

"Because I said so." Speaking with a certain tone was almost always enough, but if the kids failed to do their chores, or they committed the crime of whining or complaining about it, they faced the

consequences. Was complaining about cleaning their room worth a red bottom? Only once.

As the kids got older, their list of chores got longer. They started helping around the house and yard, sorting laundry, walking the dog, raking, weeding, skimming leaves out of the pool, taking out the garbage. No one liked that one because you took your life into your hands doing battle with Connecticut's commando raccoons.

I happen to believe that chores can be therapeutic, and kids thrive when they have a sense of personal responsibility and a clear understanding of what's expected of them. Why should kids get out of bed before noon if they don't have to? If their palms are covered with cash whenever they put their hand out, why develop ambition to earn it? Motivation comes from associating effort with reward. My father instilled it in me when I was six years old and had to wake up at dawn to get to the pool to do laps. I didn't know any other way to exist. The sooner you instill the drive to succeed in your children, the better. I taught them that if you do nothing, you get nothing. But the harder you work, the bigger the payoff. The formula isn't magic. It's how the world spins.

At thirteen, Donny was a dock attendant at the marina I built at Trump Castle, tying up boats, running supplies, gassing up, and doing whatever the marina master asked him to do. The *Trump Princess* was docked there, and we'd put high rollers on the boat for cruises to entertain them. Don assisted the guests, stocked the supplies, and cleaned up afterward. He loved boats. During our vacation weeks on my yacht each summer, he scraped barnacles off the hull and swabbed the decks. He would get so tan by the end of the month!

Both boys did landscaping on Trump properties, trimming hedges, mowing the lawns, and getting their hands dirty. It was hard work, for long hours in the summer heat, alongside men who did the same or similar work to feed their families. As Don said often on the campaign trail, "Our father had us work with the guys who had doctorates in common sense, not the guys who had doctorates in finance." Don's salary was five dollars an hour. After two years at the same rate, he finally asked his father, "Why haven't you given me a raise?"

Donald said, "You didn't ask!"

If you want something, you have to ask for it. No one is going to hand you a dollar. Don got his raise to six bucks an hour, but that life lesson was far more valuable.

When Donald was a boy, his father, Fred, brought him to construction sites, too. If Fred saw a nail on the ground, he'd pick it up and give it to the construction workers and say, "We can use this." Donald learned how to build as a boy with his father, and the tradition carried on when Donald brought Don, Ivanka, and Eric to sites when they were small. They were like his ducklings, following him around. Ivanka has joked that one of her special skills is navigating a construction site in stiletto heels. They got another education listening to Donald interact with the workers and seeing how things got done.

ERIC

Don and I did stone work, marble work, and tile work; ran electrical conduits; did plumbing; cut down trees; cut rebar with acetylene torches; ran backhoes and bulldozers; mowed yards with big tractors; and renovated properties

under my father's guidance. That's how we got our foundation in business.

A lot of the work was at Seven Springs, a property in
Westchester with a main house built by Eugene Meyer,
the chairman of the Federal Reserve and publisher of the
Washington Post, and a smaller house built by H. J. Heinz,
of Heinz ketchup. Don and I renovated the mansions
under the supervision of tough Italian contractors Vinnie
Stellio and Frank Sanzo. I woke up at six thirty a.m. and
was on the job site with a sledgehammer in my hands by
seven. Don and I lived in a caretaker's house on the property that dated back to the 1900s. He had one room and I
had the other. Our schedule: wake up, work, have lunch,
work, have dinner, go to sleep.

Don, Ivanka, and I grew up working together and then
joined forces at the Trump Organization as adults. Sharing the common objective at the office bonded us in a big
way. We worked together to grow the company all over the
world, opening hotels. We also traveled together exten-
sively and filled our free time together. Until Ivanka moved
to Washington, our three offices were side by side by side.

While the boys toiled at Seven Springs, Ivanka had another job
that paid a bit more. After doing a stint as the fourteen-year-old
host of the Miss Teen USA pageant, she landed an agent at Elite,
a modeling agency. Her first magazine shoot was for the cover of
Seventeen in 1996; soon after, she went on to pose for Tommy Hil-
figer and Sassoon jeans in advertisements, and to walk the runway

for Paco Rabanne, Marc Bouwer, and Versace. Modeling was Ivanka's way to make her own money and get away from her boarding school, Choate Rosemary Hall in Wallingford, Connecticut, which she started in tenth grade. (I initially considered Le Rosey, a private school with campuses in Rolle and Gstaad, Switzerland, but I hated it on sight. I was completely turned off by the teenagers in Armani suits smoking in the corridors, driving Mercedes, and flashing platinum cards.)

Unlike her brothers, who adored their years at the Hill School in rural Pennsylvania, Ivanka was bored at Choate. (I don't think it was academically rigorous enough for her.) At first, the dean didn't approve of her leaving campus for modeling gigs, but she fought for it by reminding administrators that they let another student, a professional skier, travel for work. They had no choice but to let her go. However, I forbade her from missing classes for modeling, so she could only work on weekends and vacations. It was better for her to earn some money and learn the ways of the world than go to nightclubs and pot parties anyway.

I never worried about her safety in the vicious modeling world because she had her head on straight and was armed with the advice I gave her. I told her that photographers will promise you everything and then try to take advantage of you. When I was a model in Czechoslovakia and Canada, a lot of my friends were used and abused. They felt pressure to do drugs with photographers and to stay thin. I also warned her to watch her back around the other girls, who would often try to sabotage you to get the job instead of you. It's a cutthroat business at every level, but she wanted to do it and I let her while keeping a very close eye on her. She was a minor and couldn't make a move without my approval. Her agent told me which magazines and designers wanted to have meetings with her or hire her, and if it was someone I didn't like or trust, I canceled it. I went to some of her shows, and if I couldn't make it to Paris, my friends looked after her. A lot of models blow all their money on clothes and the high life. Not Ivanka. She saved every penny of her income.

Back in 1991, I was in the middle of my divorce, and my friend Thierry Mugler, a gifted designer, asked me to be the muse for his haute couture collection in Paris. I needed the distraction and was flattered to be asked, so I said yes. I opened the show, and as soon as I walked onstage, the audience freaked out. It felt good to show myself in public again after a year in virtual seclusion. The show was a great success for Thierry and me. My confidence was restored, and he got a ton of glowing press. Several years later, he asked me to be in another of his collections and extended an invitation to Ivanka, too. She agreed, and in 1997, when Ivanka was sixteen, my daughter and I had the privilege of doing a runway show together.

―――――――――――――― IVANKA ――――――――――――――

Thierry was all about extravagance and high drama in his clothes; everything was very theatrical. It was a departure from how I was rolling at boarding school at the time, wearing almost exclusively cords and Birkenstocks. All of a sudden, I found myself in platform stilettos and a black patent-leather catsuit. I was so nervous—and pretty uncomfortable! I was sitting there in this full-body leather glove, fretting about tripping in those heels and falling on my face on the runway. Meanwhile, my mom was in the makeup chair next to me, totally relaxed, like it was just another day at the office.

Doing the show with her was amazing. It was an extension of something we'd always bonded over, but this time, we weren't just watching. We were in it together.

I thought Ivanka might stick with modeling, so we started looking for an apartment in Paris for her to live in during Fashion Week and photo shoots. A few days before I closed on a place, Ivanka called me to say that modeling had been fun, but she was going to stop to focus on her studies in college. I said, "Okay, sweetie. Whatever you want." As soon as we hung up, I immediately called my broker and said, "Stop the sale!" Ivanka's phone call saved me a lot.

She ended her modeling at the right time. Fashion was a fun diversion, but it wasn't going to be her career. She had bigger dreams for herself.

- 22 -

MOMS WHO DATE

I wasn't a nun after Donald and I divorced. Far from it. I love men and enjoy their attention and companionship. I was still a young woman, only forty-two, with half of my life (at least) ahead of me.

I met my second husband, Riccardo Mazzucchelli, a divorced Italian, at the horse races at Ascot in England a year and a half after the separation in 1991, and liked him right away. He was charming, with piercing blue eyes and a killer smile, but I wasn't ready to jump into a relationship. I was busy starting up House of Ivana, being a mother, and looking for a new home in Manhattan. Riccardo tried to win me over by sending me a room full of red roses, but I kept him at arm's length for a while. We'd meet for a drink here and there, but we didn't kiss until our *fifteenth* date. Instead, we walked the streets of Rome and London at night to gaze at the moon and stars. We rode around St. Moritz in a horse and carriage and walked hand in hand through the old city in Prague.

It truly was romantic—the stuff of novels.

In fact, my novel *For Love Alone* was inspired in part by Riccardo. When Lifetime made a movie of it, he stood next to me for my cameo. He also had a split second of screen time in *The First Wives Club*, the Goldie Hawn, Diane Keaton, and Bette Midler block-buster, when I delivered the line, "Don't get mad, get everything."

The first time he proposed, Riccardo gave me a beautiful dia-mond, but I said no. I didn't need a husband. I already had a family, a career, and my own money. I did need and want love and friend-ship (and sex), which Riccardo already gave me, and I made sure he knew how much I enjoyed his company. A few years went by, and we were still together and very much in love. When he proposed a second time, he gave me a gorgeous sapphire ring, and I said yes.

Don, Ivanka, and Eric were in my wedding to Riccardo on June 17, 1995, at the restaurant Le Cirque in the lobby of the May-fair Hotel on East Sixty-Fifth Street between Madison and Park Avenues. Thierry made my dress, which was gorgeous baby-blue satin, long-sleeved, knee-length, with a deep V and a nipped-in waist. My hat by Philip Treacy was a marvel of white satin, white feathers, and diamond-shaped mesh. Ivanka, then thirteen, wore a gold dress that was as slinky as mermaid scales. Diana Ross, Bar-bara Walters, Shirley Lord—all my friends were there. It was a cold night but very warm and loving inside.

Riccardo was instrumental in helping me rejoin the world and find happiness again after the ugly divorce. I didn't make a big deal of his being my boyfriend. I gradually and naturally worked

Riccardo into my home and life. The kids never complained or said, "But, Mom, it's too soon." They trusted me, and they knew I was cognizant of what I was doing. As long as Riccardo was nice to me, they were happy for me. He never tried to replace the kids' father or asked them to call him "Dad" or "Uncle Riccardo." He was just "Riccardo." He respected their relationships with Donald, and like me, he never said a bad word about him in front of the kids. From day one, they saw Riccardo as a friend—not exactly a father figure, but a grown man who loved to cook and laugh, someone to talk to and play sports with.

We bought a house at 16 Cadogan Square in London, formerly owned by a carpet mogul. The outside entrance had iron French doors, and the house had a huge master bedroom, a lovely staircase, a living room overlooking Cadogan Square, a library, and a leopard room, with spotted upholstery and wallpaper and feline art. I have one in every house. I guess I identify with the strength of the leopard. We split our time between New York and London, so Riccardo could be close to his son, Fedele.

Fedele, whom I called Deli, was Riccardo's adult son from his previous marriage. A heavyset young man, Deli was in his early twenties when we met. After his apartment in Japan burned down (not sure what happened there), Deli flew to London, where he had a seizure, was hospitalized, and was put in a straitjacket. He had a long history of erratic and destructive behavior, and during that hospitalization, he was finally diagnosed with schizophrenia. He was given medication, and if he forgot or chose not to take it, it could send him flying out of control. He used his black-belt karate skills to flip tables and break the furniture in restaurants. Once, he grabbed his father by the throat in front of me. I yelled at him to release Riccardo, and he did. Deli was a little afraid of me.

My children were afraid of Deli, and with good reason. Once, Riccardo, my kids, Deli, and I went to Greenwich together. Deli had ten years and fifty pounds on Don, who was fifteen or sixteen at the time. The kids were outside running around on the lawn, and God only knows why but Deli chased Don, caught him, threw him to the ground, jumped on top of him, and choked him. Don fought him off and told me what had happened. I freaked out and told Riccardo to keep his son away from my kids. He took Deli back to London, and he was never near my children again.

Poor Don. He really got the brunt of everything. The broken leg as a toddler, getting spanked more than the others. He was old enough to really suffer during the divorce. He had to shoulder the responsibility of finding Bridget after her heart attack. And then the near choking by his unstable stepbrother. No wonder Don likes to go in the woods and escape from everything.

Deli's doctors were in London, and Riccardo rightly felt he needed to be there for his son; Deli's Japanese wife, who was dying of brain cancer; and Deli's baby daughter (and my goddaughter), Katrina. I felt that I needed to stay in New York to raise my kids and grow my business. We tried to see each other as often as possible. In an effort to keep connected, I made him a partner at Ivana Inc., and he became more and more obsessed with my home shopping business. He pushed me to put in more hours and do more to sell my products. Then he tried to fire my financial people and company staffers I trusted, saying that they weren't loyal to me. I felt like I was fighting battles with my husband to protect my staff, and the stress just built up to the point where I couldn't have him in the office or at home. My assistant came over and we packed up his luggage and locked him out of the town house. He went back to London and that was that. After six years together and twenty months as husband and wife, we divorced in 1997.

There was just too much baggage and stress working against us, and eventually his family tragedy and our rocky business partnership drove a wedge between us. He had to be in London for his son and granddaughter. I had to be in New York for my kids and business. It was a shame, and a relief, that we had to part. I didn't grieve afterward very much. After all the turmoil, I enjoyed the peace.

We remain good friends—I'm friends with all of my exes. To this day, he's monumentally supportive of his son and granddaughter. They all live in Croatia; Riccardo bought Deli, who is doing better, an apartment in Split. I went to visit him last year to see a new resort that Riccardo opened. He's a decent man and we had a great relationship, until we didn't.

A couple of years after Riccardo and I got divorced, I met Roffredo Gaetani di Laurenzana dell'Aquila d'Aragona Lovatelli, an Italian prince, count, and duke from Rome. We met in Monaco in 1998. I hated Monaco. It's a sunny place for shady people who want to avoid paying taxes, and, at least then, it was filthy! The big cruise ships would come in and dump their garbage in the ocean right outside the city. I had a friend there who water-skied and was always having trouble with her breathing. I told her, "It's because you go into the garbage water!"

I was there that year for the Grand Prix, a Formula One auto race through the city. One of my best friends, Italian jet-setter

Massimo Gargia, had a big party on the terrace of the Hôtel de Paris and I went with eight guests, including a man I'll call Gary, a wealthy American who was after me like crazy. Massimo introduced me to Roffredo, the president of Ferrari Long Island. He was handsome and tall, from an important family (Giovanni "Gianni" Agnelli, owner of Fiat, was like an uncle to him), and single. Massimo sat Roffredo and me next to each other at the main table and banished Gary to Siberia on the other side of the room. Gary was furious!

Roffredo and I hit it off, and I invited him to join some of my friends and me on my yacht for a trip to Cap Ferrat the next day to rendezvous with a Swedish friend of mine named Henrik, a tall, blond-haired, blue-eyed man mountain. About five minutes before we shipped off, Roffredo showed up and jumped aboard. Gary was so angry to see him, he left in a huff and never set foot on my yacht again. (He didn't need to: he turned around and bought his own yacht and rented it to my friend Clive Davis.)

At Cap Ferrat, Henrik came in on his sailboat to meet us and have lunch. I sat between Roffredo, a slim, dark Italian, and Henrik, a huge Viking, and wondered, *Which one shall I choose?* As is often the case with Trumps, the decision came down to location, location, location. Henrik lived in Zurich. Over my dead body would I live there! But Roffredo lived in New York, so I thought, *I'll give him a chance.*

After our first date, Roffredo sent me a case of Brunello di Montalcino from his family vineyard. But when the case arrived, there was no note. I didn't know who to send a thank-you to! We bumped into each other a few months later and he asked, "How'd you like the wine?"

"That was you?"

Any confusion over how we felt about that first date was cleared up, and we had dinner the next night . . . and were inseparable for the next five years. He had a house on East Sixty-Third between Fifth and Madison, and I lived at East Sixty-Fourth Street one block away. After several months, he moved in with me.

Roffredo was a fabulous guy and a great lover, fun and intelligent, really gorgeous, with big shoulders and a small waist. Riccardo had a smaller build than Roffredo, and Donald was chubbier. I can always tell when Donald's weight goes up and down between 235 and 215. But Roffredo, a boxer, never gained a pound. He was lean and muscled. Being in shape was important to him, and to me. His style, though, needed some help. Roffredo hung out at Cipriani downtown with his Italian friends who all wore jogging suits, jeans, and T-shirts. I said, "If you want to go out with me, you need real clothes." Some of his father's custom-made Italian suits were hanging in Roffredo's closet, so he started wearing them. They fit him like a glove. Before long, he was named one of the best-dressed men in France.

There was conflict, as there always is. Gianni Agnelli, Roffredo's "uncle," was very possessive of him. Gianni's only son, Edoardo, jumped off a bridge in Turin and killed himself not long after Roffredo and I started seeing each other. Edoardo was a troubled soul. He'd been rejected and neglected by his father, and became a heroin addict and a religious convert, obviously searching for something he never found. After the suicide, Gianni seemed determined to break up Roffredo and me to have his "new son" all to himself.

I would plan our vacation in Corsica, and on the same dates, Gianni, who was also Roffredo's boss, would demand that he go to a meeting in Sicily. If I went to Sicily with him, Gianni would say, "Now I need you in Bastia." He did it on purpose to sabotage our relationship out of jealousy. Gianni would invite us to St. Moritz to his chalet for dinner, and he'd seat me next to him and Roffredo opposite us. Meanwhile, Gianni's long-suffering, cheated-on wife, Marella, was banished to a table across the room. He would ask me question after question to try to pick my brain about people I knew. Gianni loved to get the gossip on people and use it as ammunition against them. He got nothing from me. I never liked him. The whole Agnelli family acted like the kings and queens of Europe, with their palace intrigues and lording over others. When Gianni died in 2003, I didn't shed a tear.

Unlike Donald, a workaholic, Roffredo was a bon vivant. He shared my excitement about life and enthusiasm for adventure. He took me to the Ferrari factory in Italy once. I drove a Formula One around the track and punched it to two hundred miles per hour. He was amazed by my love for speed, but he should have known. He'd watched me ski in Aspen (I tried to teach him, but he was okay, not great). As a gift, he gave me a customized candy-red Ferrari F355 Spider, which I think is the sexiest car ever made.

Christmas 2005, I was in Aspen with the kids. Roffredo went to visit his mother, Countess Loraine Montalcino, in Tuscany. His flight landed in Rome at seven thirty a.m., and he got a rental car at eight thirty a.m. to drive to the vineyard. Two years before, while making the same drive, Roffredo had skidded off the road in the thick morning fog and crashed. I always worried about that drive and breathed a sigh of relief whenever he called to say he'd arrived safely. That year, I got a call from Italy as expected, but it wasn't

Roffredo. Loraine told me he he'd skidded off the road again in the frost and broken his neck and passed away.

I was in my suite at the Little Nell, the phone against my cheek, listening to his mother sobbing. The countess told me the funeral was the next day, but I was snowed in and couldn't go. I was devastated. Friends called all day long. Roffredo's sisters called. The phone didn't stop ringing. I know I spoke to people and listened to them try to console me. The kids were there, but what could they do?

Roffredo was only fifty-two, bursting with energy and full of joy. I cry whenever I think about him, even now, writing this chapter. I have no idea why I didn't marry him.

For a while, I was in shock. After shock came anger. *Why didn't he drive slower? Why didn't he wait until the fog lifted?* And then, once the anger subsided, my steely resolve emerged, as it always has: "I have to get on with my life." At one point during our five years together, he bought a duplex downtown near Cipriani, one of our usual spots, that I helped him decorate. I went down there and sat alone among his things, the boxing bag downstairs, his art, his clothes, and cried. I replayed my favorite memories and some mundane ones—our picking out the drapes, having drinks at the table, dancing. Grieving in his apartment was as much catharsis as I was going to get. After a few months, one of his relatives came to New York to clean out the place and sell it.

During my mourning period, I kept up with my business, my travel plans, and my activities. Otherwise, it would have been like giving up. Life can wear you down, but you can't hide from it. I'd lost two loves to divorce and two to tragic accidents, but I was still here. The world continued to spin, and I was a part of it.

The kids were all in their mid- to late twenties by then. They tried to help by taking me to lunch and coming by the town house, but there was nothing anyone could do. You have to grieve in your own way and on your own terms. I think they saw it as an opportunity to pay me back for all the support and comfort I'd given them during tough times, but that didn't feel right for me. It was my job to help them, not the other way around. I am always happy to see my kids and I appreciated the visits. But I mourned alone.

A year later, in 2006, my yacht was parked at Cannes for the film festival, and I was having a party with two hundred people on it. Massimo asked if he could bring a guest and I said, "Of course." The guest turned out to be a young, nice, very good-looking, trim, stylish man with a great sense of humor named Rossano Rubicondi, also from Rome. Clearly, I have a thing for Italians. Maybe I was Italian in a previous life.

Rossano and I got along very well, and the next day, he asked me to lunch. We started seeing each other. At the end of the summer, I invited him to cruise with me from Saint-Tropez to Sardinia. Per protocol, he gave his passport to my stewardess Anna for the captain, Alberto, to give to customs officials in San Remo. When Anna gave me the passports back, I took a peek at Rossano's date of birth. He'd told me that he was in his thirties, but he was actually twenty-nine. I almost fainted. I thought, *What am I doing?* I was *fifty*-seven.

Then again, why *not* date a much younger man? What was the alternative? Being with an old man? I'd rather be a babysitter than

a nursemaid. Take care of someone's bad knees and bad back? Forget it. If the man has other things to offer besides experience and
wealth, the relationship could be balanced. Rossano was young,
gorgeous, had some money, traveled with me, went to lunches and
dinners, took me to the airport, schlepped my luggage, and drove
me around. I prefer to go out with someone on my arm. As long
as I could afford it, I would take care of Rossano. You always have
to watch over your shoulder and tune in to any suspicious requests,
but Rossano never asked me for anything. He was just there for me,
and we had a great time together.

I didn't discuss my relationships with the kids. They were out of
the house and busy in their own lives by then. They rarely came to
Saint-Tropez anymore and didn't get to know Rossano. When they
found out about him, they didn't react positively or negatively to his
being so much younger. They might've worried that he was a gold
digger, but I assured them I wasn't concerned about that. As long as
I was happy, that's all they cared about.

Rossano and I had some good times together. One Halloween,
Nikki and I went to Trashy Lingerie in Los Angeles and got sexy
costumes for Donna and Dick Soloway's party that year. I got a
very cute Little Bo Peep costume, with a frilly white shirt with
puffy sleeves, a short skirt with a crinoline underneath, a German-
style vest, and a shepherd's crook. Rossano came up with the idea
of dressing up as Donald Trump, with a wig, the fake tan, and a
business suit. He looked so much like him, people were coming
up to us, asking when we got back together! We won first prize for
best costume.

Rossano was an excellent tennis player and he competed in the

Mar-a-Lago membership tournaments. One year, in the finals, it was Rossano versus Donald, and Rossano won. (Donald wasn't so happy about that.) His name is on a plaque in Mar-a-Lago for that win, etched in copper.

After two years together, we decided to get married at Mar-a-Lago in the ballroom, a space big enough for our six hundred guests, and Donald was kind enough to waive the $20,000 fee. All I had to pay for was the food and drink, and the décor. After doing five thousand weddings at the Plaza, I knew exactly what I wanted and who I wanted involved to put the magical day together.

The Friday afternoon before the ceremony, Maryanne Trump, Donald's sister, the judge who was officiating, asked for my marriage license.

I said, "Our . . . oh, shit."

We completely forgot to get it! Rossano and I got into an SUV and drove to the courthouse in West Palm Beach, but there were five hundred people in line ahead of us. We tried going into another office, the department of criminal justice or something, and asked if we could get a marriage license there. The woman behind the desk looked at me and said, "Hi, Ivana. What can I do for you?" I explained the situation to her. She said that, to get married in Florida, you have to get a license three days before the event, and it has to be approved by a judge. *But* if we had an address in another state, she could give us one that day. I told her, "Name it, I've got it," and gave her my address in New York.

She made out the waiver. "That'll be seventy-two dollars," she said. "Cash only."

Rossano and I emptied our pockets. I had a fifty, and he had twenty-two exactly. We just made it. The irony of it: I was throwing a ridiculously expensive wedding, and we were counting out quarters to get the license the day before. When we finally left the courthouse, we were starving from not eating all day. "Can you wait?" he asked me. The rehearsal dinner was starting with cocktails around the pool at five p.m., and later on, there would be a decadent meal and dancing.

My eyes were crossing from hunger. "I can't," I said. We found an ATM and went to a hot dog stand outside the courthouse. Rossano bought what seemed like twenty of them, and we sat down on the steps and ate them all. That night, I wore a Bob Mackie beaded, pearled dress that was so heavy, I couldn't walk in it. I had to sit on one of the couches around the pool and wait for my guests to come to me. It was a beautiful evening, with a hanging moon and sparkling stars.

The next morning, we got hitched. The wedding party was huge. Twenty-five bridesmaids in pastel shades walked side by side with twenty-five groomsmen in white, and they ascended twin staircases on either side of the altar. First, the flower girls dropped rose petals down the aisle. Then Ivanka, my maid of honor, came down in a yellow dress. Don and Eric walked with me in my pink Zuhair Murad dress. Donald stood by the swimming pool to watch the ceremony, led by his sister. He attended dinner and had a good time. I sat him at a table with his business friends.

For the reception, we had to fit eighty tables in the ballroom, each one covered in lace tablecloths with unbelievable flowers. Waiters in white gloves and tuxedos served a gourmet dinner that included caviar, foie gras, and lamb. Rossano entered the room to the *Rocky* theme. Our first dance? A tango to a song from *Damn Yankees*, "Whatever Lola Wants," but Rossano sang to me, "Whatever Ivana wants . . ." I'd changed into a long hot-pink dress with a feather tail, so the dancing wasn't so easy for me. I was worried I'd get tangled in the tail. I was so busy chatting with our guests, I didn't eat a thing. Rossano had a ball, jumping up on the stage and singing with the band. All the kids made a speech for us. Don's was the funniest. He said, "Mom, Rossano, I wish you all the best. And, Rossano, if you ever do anything to our mother, we are in the construction business and we know how to bury the bodies."

By three p.m., the wedding was over, but we still had the daunting task of going through ten thousand shots of the event as part of our exclusive rights deal with Getty, the photo agency that was selling the pictures to the media. I changed into a jogging suit, and we plowed into the job, finishing fourteen hours later (with a few short breaks) at six a.m. We hadn't eaten all day (again), not even a nibble. The kitchen was closed, so we drove to West Palm Beach and bought day-old sandwiches at a 7-Eleven and ate them. Some wedding feast! Then we drove back to Concha Marina and went to bed.

Before the wedding, I admit, I had second thoughts. I had a great prenup, so I was protected financially, but, as much fun as we had together, I wondered if he was using me. After the wedding, we didn't go for a honeymoon. He went to Miami and I went to France, and we didn't see each other for a while. While in Saint-Tropez, a very small town, I learned that Rossano had a girlfriend, a Cuban girl he'd met in Miami and brought to France. This was only a couple of months after the wedding!

It stung. I wouldn't call it a deep cut, though. By this point, I'd been down this road before and had the experience and wisdom to get over it quickly. I filed for divorce and was free within a year. It was very quiet. No publicity. No acrimony. I just couldn't be married to a cheater again or be bound to a user. But I genuinely like and care about Rossano, and after some time apart to get over the hurt feelings, we became good friends, and still are today. He's opening up a pizza place in West Palm Beach near Mar-a-Lago, and I wish him the best of luck. I've known him for over ten years. He's like family.

But what's a mature woman with an attraction to younger men to do? I'm certainly not going to marry a man who cheats or tries to control me. Since men are men, and many men cheat and control, I don't see another marriage in my future. But romance and fun will always be a part of my life. Right now, I'm seeing a few (young) men, and enjoying their companionship and sense of humor very much.

BAN ON BRATS, COUCH POTATOES, AND DRUGGIES

Don went to college at Donald's alma mater, the Wharton School at the University of Pennsylvania in Philadelphia, and Eric went on to Georgetown University in Washington, DC, and had a great time there.

Ivanka also went to Georgetown University, and perfected her French, Italian, and Czech. After two years, she told me she wanted to transfer to Wharton to concentrate on business classes. She made the switch and graduated from there two years later with honors.

When the kids went to college, I saw a lot less of them, which was the downside. The upside for them: they were shielded from the press. Sending them away was their best chance for a close-to-normal life. I would go visit them for Parents' Weekends or for special occasions, but I was busy working and traveling. They had their studies and social lives. Donald and I split holidays and spring and summer breaks. During their last teen years, whole months could go by without my seeing my children.

I wasn't worried that, without my constant presence, they'd automatically turn to drugs and alcohol. But I was concerned that if they befriended one bad apple, it could undo years of solid parenting. Say they started hanging out with druggies and drunks and were lured into slacking off and wasting themselves? I'd put too much into my kids to see it all fall apart because of some loser. It was my deepest fear, what I prayed wasn't going to happen.

At the beginning of each semester, if my schedule allowed, I went to the kids' colleges and took their friends and roommates to lunch. A lot of parents did the same thing, but I wasn't offering just to be nice. I was conducting a stealth interrogation. It wasn't at the same level as the Soviet secret police, but I did a thorough job. I could tell in fifteen minutes if one of my kids' roommates or friends was a bad influence. My checklist:

1. **Do they smoke?** None of these kids would dare smoke in front of me, but I can tell if someone is a smoker if they are within ten feet of me. My nose is very sensitive. Cigarettes or pot, I can sniff it out.

2. **Do they drink?** Again, if a high school or college kid ordered a glass of wine or beer at lunch with me, I would have hit the roof. No way! These were smart kids, and none was so stupid as to try that. (But if I wanted a glass of wine, I certainly would have one.)

3. **Are they late?** You know how I feel about lateness. Being late for lunch? Forget it. They'll be late with homework, too, and might slack off about graduating on time, or try to get my kids to put off their deadlines, too.

4. **Are they rude?** Manners are even more important to me. Kids who didn't say "please" and "thank you," look me in the eye, and have proper table manners (napkin in lap, waiting for everyone to be served before eating, etc.) were not going to cut it with me. If they were rude or impolite to a waiter? The worst!

5. **Are they lazy?** Taking extra classes, playing sports, and being active in clubs, student government, and the arts? Fabulous! Busy kids with full lives don't have time to slip off track. But slackers who coast in class and don't have anything better to do than smoke pot on the couch? Nope.

My strategy was to speak to them like a normal parent, but the whole time, I was picking their brains. I asked about their class schedules and activities. I looked at how they ate. Were they sloppy? Did they order unhealthy, fried, greasy food? Did they listen or interrupt when other people spoke? I asked what they did with their time, what their goals were, what they loved to do. If they couldn't answer me with enthusiasm and passion, I had to wonder if they were trouble.

I watched it all. I registered every morsel of information I could find. For the most part, I liked all of my kids' friends. But if something didn't seem right, you better believe I called the school and asked for a roommate switch. I was always polite and respectful, but I got my point across.

I'm sure the kids hated that about me. School was their chance to get away from Trumpland and all the influence and pressure that came with it. They needed to carve out their own lives and identities apart from us. Their desire to be independent was proof they were growing up. I didn't want to squash that by calling and interfering, but maybe I wasn't as ready as they were to let go.

Don especially set out to bury his identity as a rich kid. His first year at the Hill School, I drove him to Pennsylvania in the limo, which he found embarrassing enough. It was the end of our brutal year—the separation, our seclusion at Mar-a-Lago, the summer on the move. Don was ready to stay in one place, away from the paparazzi and the city, to be just a normal kid among other normal kids. We spent the afternoon walking around the campus and setting up his room. He was polite and patient, but I could tell he wanted me to go. I wasn't ready to say good-bye to him just yet. It'd be the last I'd see of him until Thanksgiving (or so I thought; we'd see each other in just a month when my father died). I said, "Let's go out to dinner!"

He said, "Okay, Mom, but not here. Let's go to the next town over."

"Why?"

"Because other families will be having dinner in town and if I walk into a restaurant with you, they'll all know who my parents are." They'd figure it out eventually, but he wanted to delay the inevitable.

He wasn't ashamed of Donald and me. He just wanted to be treated like everyone else, which I understood. We took the limo to a neighboring town and the only place to go was a Taco Bell.

We walked in. I really did try not to be obviously me. I smiled at the man behind the counter and said, "We'll have . . . tacos, please. That seems to be your *espécialité*. And I'd like a glass of Chablis, too. Thank you."

The man blinked at me. "Chablis?"

"Yes, white wine, please."

"Um, we have Coke, Pepsi . . ."

FYI: they don't serve wine at Taco Bell. One learns new things every day.

The bill came and it was $15 for a plastic tray of tacos and soda. All I had on me was a $100 bill. I gave it to the man behind the counter and he looked at me like I'd just fallen off the moon. They didn't have enough cash in the register to make change, so our driver had to go find someplace that would break a hundred.

We sat down to eat, and Don and I just started laughing. The joke was on me—what do I know about Taco Bell?—but laughing with him, just the two of us with the plastic tray at the table bolted to the floor, was a real moment. It was a relief. He was escaping city stress and starting over with some level of anonymity. It was his chance to be his own young man. I would miss him, but he needed to be away. I understood.

Unfortunately, the next day, our picture was in the paper. The headline on the full-page article and photo was something like, "Ivana Trump Eats at Taco Bell!" Oh, well. Don's chance to be "normal" didn't last long.

The same thing happened a year later, when Donald and I took him back for his second year at the Hill together. We drove in the limo, which Don was as uncomfortable about as always. When we walked with him to his dorm room, I realized I'd forgotten to pack some essentials—bedsheets, extra towels, and shampoo. Donald and I left Don at school and drove to the nearest place, a Kmart, to buy what he needed. The next day, a photo ran on the cover of the *New York Post* with the headline "Guess Who Shops at Kmart."

When I took Eric to the Hill for his first day, we made sure he had everything he needed in one big suitcase. Everyone looked shocked, as if they assumed he didn't go anywhere without twenty pieces of matching Vuitton luggage. Poor Eric. He had to carry a lot of baggage, yes, just not a lot of luggage.

TRAVEL MAKES YOU RICH

Like education and the arts, travel is an expenditure that makes you rich. The more you spend, the wealthier you are. As a mother and as a European, I felt it was essential to show my children where I came from and for them to be able to speak at least two or three languages. I speak Czech, Russian, and English fluently, as well as some French, Italian, and German. To be a citizen of the world, you have to see it and be able to communicate with different people. Every summer when the kids were young, they'd visit my mother in the Czech Republic at her city house in Zlín and her country chalet.

—————————————————— ERIC ——————————————————

The first floor of the chalet had a living room with a hard-wood table, two benches with a table in between them, a wood-burning stove, and a tiny four-by-four kitchen. No TV. No computer. It was totally isolated. To get to the second floor, you had a pull-down ladder into an attic. The only thing up there was a handmade goose-down mattress. My grandparents slept on it. When we were little, we'd all pile in and hang out up there.

After my grandfather died, it was just Babi, Ivanka, Don, and me in that simple, beautiful house for several weeks at a stretch. We'd play in the woods all day, build things, go hiking, and figure out how to entertain ourselves. At night, we'd make a fire in the stove and play cards—gin rummy and war. We'd crash, and then wake up the next morning and do it all again.

After their time with their grandmother, they'd come cruising with me in the Mediterranean. We motored to Monaco for the Grand Prix, Portofino, Rome, Venice, Capri, Positano on the Amalfi Coast, Sicily, Corsica, Sardinia, Saint-Tropez, Turkey, Greece, and Croatia, and anchored to snorkel, fish with lines and spears, visit villages, cook together, and enjoy the good life. We'd say, "Where next?" and then we'd go. We were incredibly fortunate to be able to see the world this way, and I made sure the kids knew how lucky they were to get to experience such pleasures.

For most of the nineties, Riccardo was the man in my life, and the captain of *Stilyani III*, a sixty-five-foot yacht. It was two stories high, and we'd jump off the top platform into the sea. Riccardo was great in the water and taught the kids how to snorkel and where to find the best fish. In Corsica, he knew every hot spot. He'd dive down with gloves and a knife to cut the sea urchins off the rocks and bring them back up for lunch. He'd cut them open, and I'd put a drop of champagne in each one. The kids didn't like them at first. It is an acquired taste, but you grow to love it.

We always stopped at Cavoli Beach on Elba, a very popular beach for kids, and go snorkeling all the way to the far edges of the swimming area. One time, there was a huge eel wrapped around the pole of the warning sign. Riccardo grabbed the spear gun and killed it, and we brought it back to the yacht. The kids and I were totally grossed out but laughing hysterically as he cleaned and cooked it. It was awful! A mushy, overcooked mess.

Another time, we anchored in Ponza, an island in Italy, to water-ski and snorkel. The kids decided that they wanted spaghetti and meatballs for dinner, so we went into the tiny village to a butcher and bought ground sirloin. Bad choice. You need more fat in beef for meatballs. We tried to eat them, but they were hard as rocks. I put them in a Ziploc baggie in the fridge. The next day, while the kids were swimming, I snuck up behind them and emptied the meatballs into the water. Then I screamed, "Kids! Get out of the water! There's poop all over the place!" They scrambled back on the boat in ten seconds flat. It was hilarious! Practical jokes were a big thing on the yachts. Don once swam under and attached his fishhook to the bottom of the boat and then pretended like he had a monster on the line. Eric tried to reel in the yacht for ten minutes before he realized what Don had done.

At the end of one summer, we were anchored off Sardinia to get one more day of swimming before the kids and I had to go back to New York. It was starting to get dark, so I called the kids in, and we weighed anchor. But something wasn't right. We couldn't find the lights of the harbor entrance. We drove very slowly in the pitch blackness looking for it, and then *boom!* Riccardo hit a rock and the boat ended up on top of it. We were stuck in uncharted waters in the dark, teetering on a rock.

We didn't know what to do. It was possible the hull had been punctured and the boat was sinking. Of course, I thought, *Radio for help!* But if you call for a rescue and are towed to port, the rescuer can claim ownership of a portion of the boat. So the plan was to go to the tender (the small boat attached by a rope to the yacht, to use for traveling from ship to shore) until we figured out what was happening and see if we could do anything about it.

I said to Ivanka, "Go get dressed." I meant for her to just throw something over her bathing suit, but she went to her cabin and packed up her entire suitcase, in case she needed her party dress or toothbrush while we were stranded in the tender. Don jumped into action and immediately started helping Riccardo and the deck-hands. I went to my cabin and got my diamond ring and all of our passports. The crew helped Ivanka, Eric, and me into the tender. I was completely coolheaded, saying, "If the boat sinks, it sinks. It's the end of the season anyway." But then, as I was going down the slippery steps in the dark, I broke a nail. And *then* I totally freaked out.

We sat in the tender for an hour until a wave came and lifted the yacht off the rock. No puncture, no damage. We got back on board, and Ivanka went to unpack her suitcase. I ran to my room to perform an emergency manicure.

I bought my Cantieri di Baia–built 120-foot yacht, named *M.Y. Ivana*, in Naples in 1995 and had her for twelve years. The kids traveled with me on my floating home for a couple of summers, but then they went off to college and had their own lives and vacation plans. The last thing they wanted to do in June was to cruise around Europe with their mom and her crazy friends. I ran my yacht like a hotel, ordering supplies once a week, setting up accounts in different ports all around Europe, hiring the staff, managing maintenance. I did the sleeping and eating arrangements for the guests. I knew every noise on my boat. I could tell you which of my guests had made love the night before. (If the yacht is a-rocking, don't come a-knocking!) After Riccardo and I broke up, I bounced back by throwing tons of parties on my yacht, picking up friends in every port, just enjoying the sun and sea, and thanking my lucky stars that this was my life. I called the top deck of the yacht "the pussy platform." We'd jump off it, thirty feet into the water. All went naked, except for me. I remembered the time Jackie O. was photographed naked on the beach on Skorpios in Greece and the photo appeared all over the world. I kept my bikini on! One year, fur designer Dennis Basso came on the boat with his partner Michael, along with a handful of other friends. We made garlands and decorations, and the captain "married" Dennis and Michael (they got married for real years later). To celebrate, we all jumped off the pussy platform into the water. Dennis was the last to go, but he balked. We yelled, "Jump!" He still refused.

I said, "If you jump, I'm going to buy your sable coat!"

He never moved so fast—and made an impressive splash when he hit the water.

M.Y. Ivana was my home away from home for twelve years. We went everywhere. I fell in love with Roffredo and traveled with Rossano on it, had countless parties and nights of fun. After twenty years on Riccardo's yacht and then my own, though, I'd seen enough of the Mediterranean for a lifetime. Plus *M.Y. Ivana* was expensive to maintain and dock. I was trying to figure out what to do with it, when someone knocked on my door at Concha Marina in 2007. I sent my houseman David to open the door.

There was a couple from Texas, well dressed, middle-aged, all-American looking. The husband said, "Excuse me, but we couldn't help noticing the Ferrari in the driveway." They'd have had to be blind not to! It was a Formula One race car, bright red, with a vanity plate that said IVANA. I was never called a plain Jane, and neither were my vehicles.

"Is it for sale?" he asked.

"I'm sorry, no," David said. There was a three-year waiting list for my car, so I couldn't blame them for asking. But my Ferrari was a gift from Roffredo. I would never sell it.

The wife said, "We just came to Palm Beach, and we're looking for a place to live. Are you selling your house?"

First they wanted my car, and now my house? No. But . . . what about the boat? After consulting with me, David told them, "She's not ready to sell the house at this time, but do you want to buy a yacht?"

He took them to the marina where *M.Y. Ivana* was docked. They took a quick tour and said, "We'll take it!"

Just like that. I sold it to them without a broker. The next day, I got a check and handed them the keys.

You know what people say, that the two happiest days of a boat owner's life are the day she buys the boat and the day she sells it? That was a *very* good day.

Every June for the last forty years, I've attended the Royal Ascot horse races in Berkshire, England, a few miles from Windsor Castle, as a member of the Annabelle Goldstein Club, a very private club in London. In the late nineties, they realized they needed young blood and created a junior membership. Ivanka was the first junior member of Annabelle's, and at fifteen, she started coming to the races with me.

You don't just throw on any old thing to hobnob with the queen and the British aristocracy. The tradition is for the men to dandy up in gray suits and tails with top hats. The ladies wear garden-party cocktail dresses, high heels (that get stuck in the mud or grass), and extravagant hats. It's really all about the hats. Ivanka and I would arrive a few days before the races to meet with a milliner. She would look at what we were going to wear and design gorgeous hats with wide brims, exploding feathers, and flowers in vibrant colors to match our dresses. The races last for five days, and depending on your schedule, you might need five hats. We attended on opening day, a Tuesday; Ladies Day on Thursday; and once more during the week.

In our dresses and hats, we'd take a Rolls-Royce from my apartment in London to Windsor Castle, right next door, and park on the grass on the edge of the Ascot fields. My friend Lizz Brewer hosted a picnic lunch on the field with chairs, tents, a buffet with champagne, of course, and bottomless Pimm's cocktails—Pimm's fruit drink, seltzer, lemon, cucumber, and gin—served in silver cups. Beware the Pimm's Cup! You have one and think, *It's so sweet and harmless.* Have two or three, and you are gone. They're deadly!

After lunch, we'd take out Queen Elizabeth–approved badges to gain access to the paddocks, the "backstage" area, to see the horses, Ivanka's favorite part of the day. She loved horses from her days taking riding lessons in Greenwich. We'd always have a moment to stop at the restaurant next to the paddocks for nibbles of lobster, spiced meats, and strawberries with cream. From there, we'd pass through the gates of the arena wearing our purple carnations and badges, smiling at the photographers and press from the BBC who asked for interviews.

By this point, half the crowd was drunk, and the races hadn't even started yet. First, the royal family—Elizabeth and Philip in gold braids, Diana and Charles (and then Camilla and Charles), Andrew and the Duchess of York—rode in on horse-drawn carriages from Windsor Castle, waved at the crowds, and took their places in the queen's suites above the fray. You could sit in the grandstands or, as we preferred, stand on the grass on the same level as the track, close enough to feel the earth shake when the horses thundered past. Sometimes, I'd place a bet, but only after I'd researched the horses, trainers, and jockeys. I broke my "never gamble" rule and would put down twenty or thirty pounds to win or place or both, and won most of the time. I'd stay until the late afternoon, and have our driver pick us up to go back to London to rest and then dress for a black-tie dinner at Annabelle's.

A secondary celebration of Ascot week was the famous Grosvenor House Art and Antiques Fair. A member of the royal family would show up, give a speech, and open the show of incredible art and furniture. One June, Ivanka, Riccardo, Nikki, and I went to Grosvenor House and then to dinner at Annabelle's. We got home at one a.m. We were just getting into bed when the phone rang. "Hello. Ivana Trump, please," said the man.

"This is Ivana. Who's this?"

"Scotland Yard. We need to speak to you."

"What did I do now?" I asked.

Two detectives, a man and a woman, arrived at the door five minutes later and told us that they'd caught a gang of thieves. Under interrogation, they told the detectives that I was their next target. Somehow, they'd gotten my schedule, had been following me all week, and had planned on robbing me at Grosvenor House! They decided against it because our group was too large. Their backup plan was to wait until I got home, push me into the house, tie me up, and beat me until they got the combination for the safe.

I was horrified by the very idea of this plot. Ivanka was there with me. She was only sixteen at the time. An experience like that could have traumatized her for life. I called Laurence Graff, the English diamond jeweler, and asked, "Who is your best bodyguard?" and hired the man to sit in the lobby of my house for six months.

Several years later, we had another near miss in London. Rossano and I were in town and met Ivanka, who'd been staying at my apartment for a few days. Rossano and I went to a black-tie dinner that night, and Ivanka went directly to the airport to return to New York. When we got home later, Rossano started to get undressed and asked, "Ivana, did you move my watches?"

I hadn't touched them.

"They're gone," he said.

I ran into the bedroom and went immediately to my Louis

Vuitton jewelry box. I didn't put my diamonds in the safe when we got there, just shoved them in my lingerie drawer, assuming they'd be safe. They were gone. Only a portion of the jewelry's value was insured.

I called Scotland Yard to report the crime. "This is Ivana Trump," I said.

"You again?"

There was no forced entry or fingerprints. The detectives were on the case for a long time, but the culprits were never found. They assumed it was an inside job. One of the stolen items was a diamond-and-gold Buccellati purse. Who would think the baubles on a woman's clutch were real? The thieves had to *know*. A year later, we thought one of the stolen items, a canary-diamond Tiffany brooch in the shape of a bird, surfaced at an auction in Geneva. The detective went undercover, but it turned out to be a smaller brooch of the same design.

If Ivanka had delayed her travel by one day, she would have been home alone when the thieves came. She could have been attacked, kidnapped, or killed. Rossano had to talk me down for weeks afterward. Since that time, I've stopped traveling with jewelry. To be honest, I hardly ever wear my jewelry anymore. For one thing, dripping in diamonds makes you look old. For another, it's like wearing a sign that reads ROB ME!

I felt bad for Kim Kardashian when she was robbed in Paris last year. But then the thieves told the police that she'd made it easy for them. She posted a photo of herself on Instagram wearing her $4 million ring, and updated on Twitter where she was staying and what she was doing. I'm not blaming the victim, but the robbers themselves said that they couldn't have done the job if she hadn't given them all the information they needed. You just can't trust the whole world with sensitive information. One thing I've learned after all my years in the public eye is that you have to maintain some privacy to be safe. My children have absolutely followed my lead there. As open as they are with the media, they hold much more back than they let on.

Nowadays, the door to my house in Saint-Tropez is always (figuratively) open for the kids and their families, whether I'm there or not. Ivanka came often when she was in college, and I used to tease her for going to bed hours before I did. When Eric was in college, he went down there with a few friends and called me in New York their first night. "Mom, there's a line of two hundred people at Papagayo. Can you help us?" he asked. Le Papagayo is a popular restaurant/disco, one of my favorite nightspots, and hard to get into.

I called security at the club and said, "My son and his friends are on line outside. Can you please let him in?" I helped my eighteen-year-old son get into a club. I knew they were good kids, and it was a special occasion for him. In France, my rules for the kids are looser.

My rules for myself are, too, unless I get caught. In Saint-Tropez, I used to ride a Vespa scooter around the village to do my shopping and get some air. I rode right past the police station, and one of the young cops flagged me down. "Ivana, you don't have a helmet," he said. "You can't ride without one."

I said, "I'm sorry, I just had my hair done. It won't happen again."

The next day, I went right by the station again. And I got stopped again.

"Today, you will have to pay a fine," the cop said. "Eighty euros."

I said, "Let me go and I'll give the money to the florist who cuts my flowers or the farmer who sells me eggs. I'll spend a fortune in the market today, and I promise not to do it again."

I kept my promise and shopped up a storm. But no way was I going to put on a helmet! Instead of breaking the law, I got rid of the scooter, and now, when in the South of France, I prefer to walk. Better for the legs and my tan anyway.

PART SIX

ADVANCED PARENTING

I DON'T MEDDLE (MUCH)

Even when your kids become adults, you still worry and keep an eye on them, especially if they seem to be veering in the wrong direction.

After Don graduated from Wharton in 2000, I assumed he'd come back to New York and start working for his father's company as he had been groomed to do from childhood. But instead, he moved to Colorado. He said he wanted to live and be free in the great outdoors, not stuck in an office tower—the same one he grew up in—in the city. He took his Ivy League business degree, moved into a tiny apartment in Aspen, and got part-time jobs teaching fly-fishing and bartending at the Tippler, a rowdy watering hole at the base of the mountain.

I was totally opposed to this plan. I'd never heard the phrase "gap year," and it sounded like the stupidest thing in the world. That's some American tradition, doing nothing for a year and losing the discipline and momentum you built up in college. I told Don, "You'll become lazy. It's a waste of time." I was worried that when he decided to get a real job, he'd have forgotten everything he'd learned in school. The very idea went against all my beliefs. It was like stepping off the elevator of success to sit on your butt and let your brain turn into oatmeal. How would he ever get back on the elevator? His father disapproved, too.

Don rebelled against our wishes and said he could make his own decisions. Apparently, that meant he was going to live in the woods and shoot rabbits, whether we liked it or not. I couldn't force him to do what I thought was best, but I made my point clear by not visiting him in Colorado and cutting him off. If he was going to waste his life, he'd support himself doing it. We didn't have a heated discussion, nor did I threaten him. I just stopped sending checks. It took eighteen months, but he eventually came around to my way of thinking on his own. He quit his job in Aspen and returned to New York to take his place in the Trump Organization.

DON

I joke that I'm the first person to graduate from the Wharton School at the University of Pennsylvania to move out west to be a bartender. It was a calculated move. I felt like I needed to get stuff out of my system and make sure I didn't have any regrets before I entered the real world. I always knew that it was a temporary break between college and working at the Trump Organization. After a while, I did feel a need to use my education and return to New York.

I planned my trip home, hoping for a smooth transition from living in the country to working in the city. But that's the opposite of what happened. My first day of work was scheduled for September 17, 2001, one week after 9/11. My long drive home starting on the fifteenth gave me plenty of time to reflect on the tragedy of what happened.

While Don was planning his trip home, I was in Montreal visiting my old friend George and appearing at the opening of the philharmonic orchestra to help them raise funds. It was a short trip. I only packed one dress in my bag. After I did my thing at the concert, I invited my friends to come to my hotel suite. We had some wine and snacks, and stayed up talking and laughing until four a.m., having a good time. My flight from Montreal to New York was at nine a.m.—on September 11, 2001. I thought, *Why go to sleep at all?* I don't need a lot of sleep. High-energy people generally don't. I had the concierge rebook me on the first flight out, at seven a.m. I boarded with nothing to check and had a short, pleasant flight to LaGuardia Airport. We landed at 8:35 a.m. I got in the car to drive home, and as we were approaching the Triborough Bridge, the first plane hit the north tower at 8:46 a.m. We could see the fire and smoke from the car. Then the second plane hit the south tower at 9:03 a.m. Already the sirens and craziness had overwhelmed the city. My driver took me straight home and stayed with me. Dorothy didn't know I'd switched my flight. She was calling my hotel in Montreal, trying to tell me not to check out. I tried to call her, but landlines and cell phones were dead. She had no idea I was sitting in my living room, watching the news in disbelief and horror. We figured out later that the planes that hit the Twin Towers were in the air at the same time mine was. Roffredo was downtown, jogging along the Hudson River, and saw everything; he returned home covered head to toe in mortar and dust.

Of course, I thought about my children, even though I knew they were safe. Don was still in Colorado, Ivanka was in college, and Eric was at boarding school. They were trying frantically to reach me all day. Late that night around ten p.m., I was able to get in touch with them and Dorothy to say I was home safe.

What a horrific, traumatic time for our country. I stared at the TV for weeks afterward, and my heart broke for all the families of the victims. All over New York, people put up signs asking about the missing, who were presumed dead. The smoke and smell of the disaster lingered in the city for days and carried all the way uptown to my town house. After a long period of sadness for the loss of lives and our sense of security, my feelings turned to anger at those criminals who did this to us. I was furious that my beloved city had been scarred. I knew we'd come back stronger than ever, and we have. Unfortunately, the threat of terrorism hasn't gone away.

September 11 made me love New York even more. I think it had the same effect on the kids. Ivanka didn't bother with a gap when she graduated from Wharton in 2004. She worked for a year as a project manager at Bruce Ratner's Forest City, a real estate management and development firm, to see how business was done from a different perspective before joining her brother and father at Donald's company. Eric went directly to work alongside his siblings as soon as he graduated with honors from Georgetown in 2006 with a degree in finance and management.

And then, in a blink, the kids were no longer children. One

minute, they were babies, and the next, they were all grown up. Although I felt a little sad that that part of their lives, and mine, was over, I was proud of them and glad to see them settle in at the Trump Organization. Each one had launched into adulthood and taken to their career like they were born to it, which, in every sense, they were. All the hard work I'd put in to get them ready for a fabulous life had come to fruition, making me one happy mama.

Get the right job. Marry the right person.

These are the only two steps you need to reach your full potential. I knew the kids were at the right place professionally to learn and become builders and deal makers while working under their father's wing. The second step, though, finding and marrying the right person, wasn't quite as simple.

I have a complicated relationship with marriage, clearly. What I told my children was that you have to be in love from the beginning. Over time, you will really get to know if this person is right or wrong for you. Unfortunately, no one can say for sure that they'll be as madly in love after twenty years of marriage as they were as newlyweds. Life has too many surprises up its sleeve for guarantees like that. But hedge your bets by starting in romance and passion, and, with kindness and patience, allowing the love to grow into mutual respect and companionship. After you get married and have kids, establish a routine and shift into a friendly partnership of enjoying life together. The fact is—and I do mean the *fact*—no one who's been married for ten years has sex more than a few times a month, once a week tops. You can't count on hot sex to sustain a long-term marriage, but the chemistry that originally brought you together can turn into a meeting of minds. You have to be stimulated by your partner's brain more than anything else. I could never be with a stupid man. It's just not interesting or attractive. Donald and I had a real meeting of the minds. We used to talk for hours and hours. I hoped my kids would have the kind of relationships that began in volcanic passion that, like lava, would cool over time into something permanent and nourishing, where love and life could grow.

Don had his first girlfriend at fifteen. When I found out about her, I sat him down for the Talk. Actually, it was more like the Lecture. I told him about STDs and made him read aloud from a pamphlet about transmission a dozen times until he could recite it from memory! I hope the message got through. Apparently, he was Don Juan in college and dated a lot. I heard that his girlfriends were always the prettiest, which didn't surprise me (apple, tree). I didn't have to give the Lecture to Eric. Don took care of that for me. Ivanka knew how I felt about safe sex because she got the Lecture, too. The last thing I wanted was for her to get pregnant too young, so I told her to be *very* careful and make sure she was always protected.

When the kids started dating in earnest after college, I backed off from meddling almost completely. The boys didn't give me too much opportunity to scrutinize their girlfriends anyway. They were very private about who they were seeing and kept me in the dark. Don introduced me to only one of his girlfriends, a sporty, fun Canadian. They were close enough to adopt a black Labrador together. I liked her, but she wasn't a good fit for the Trump family. He figured that out and they broke up. She started calling me and my mother in the Czech Republic, begging us to intervene on her behalf and tell Don to take her back. It was extremely awkward. I felt sorry for her, but there was nothing I could do. "I can't force love," I told her. "If you split, you split. Get on with your own life." I hope she did, and that she's happy.

He met Vanessa Haydon, a model, actress, and tennis star from Manhattan, not long after he broke up with the Canadian. Don was at a fashion show with his father, and Donald noticed Vanessa at the start of the event (she was one of the models). He went right over to her and said, "Have you met my son?" and introduced them. At the show's intermission, Donald went back over to Vanessa again and asked, "Have you met my son?"

She said, "Um, yes. A few minutes ago."

Don and Vanessa had to be introduced for a third time at a friend's dinner party. If at first they didn't make much of an impression on each other, once they started dating, they got serious very quickly and wed within a year. I can't speak for Don, but I fell in love with Vanessa at first sight. She's the kindest, sweetest girl in the whole wide world. I was thrilled that Don was jumping in and marrying the woman he loved, not waiting for his life as a husband and (soon enough) a father to begin. The wedding was at Mar-a-Lago, officiated by Maryanne Trump. It was the first of my children's weddings, and I basked in my role as MOG (mother of the groom). It was no work, all fun.

Ivanka didn't bring many boyfriends home, either, not for her sake or mine, but for the guys'. Introducing a boyfriend to Donald and me was a terrifying experience, so she was very selective about the ones she thought could handle it.

For a few years, Ivanka dated a Wall Streeter who was generous, sweet, smart, successful—all good things. I met him at a dinner and liked everything about him, but he was only five foot five! Ivanka is six feet tall. In stilettos, she towered over him. When we had a private moment that night, she asked me, "Well? What do you think?"

I said, "I don't dislike him. I've just had it with him up to *here*," and put my hand level with my breasts, an approximation of his height. "You get it? *Up to here!*"

Hey, I thought it was funny. I waited for her to laugh along, but Ivanka did not see the humor. She didn't speak to me for two weeks.

She and the diminutive banker broke up soon after. I don't know the intimate details of why they split. Ivanka wouldn't be so superficial as to get rid of a man because he was much shorter than her, but the truth is, she'd have had to spend her whole life looking down at the top of his head. I'm sure she had good reasons for ending it. Who knows? Maybe, as they got to know each other better, she'd had it up to *here*, too.

Ivanka dated another guy, the son of a socialite with family in Palm Beach, for several years. He was very funny, charming, a certain kind of handsome that wasn't my type. I could see why Ivanka was attracted to him. But he was too cocky. We met for the first time in early March in Palm Beach at a charity cocktail party I threw at Max Mara, and she brought him along. I asked him, "What do you do?" It wasn't an interrogation, just making conversation.

He said, "I watch my parents' and grandparents' estate."

It sounded vague, but I knew what it meant to me. I felt he had no ambition, and as long as his family was rich, he'd do nothing on his own. He was the nephew of a friend of mine, and I really wanted to like him. But I couldn't see Ivanka and him together for long. Ivanka deserved the whole package: an ambitious man who looked good at her side. This cocky charmer wasn't going to make a name for himself. He seemed completely content to live off his family's money and go to parties. I pointed *that* out to her, and she didn't speak to me for two weeks again, though she broke up with him soon after.

To his credit, he did do something productive, coproducing a documentary in 2003. But other than that movie, the cocky boyfriend lived up to my doubts about him. Ten or so years after their split, he was arrested for possession of cocaine outside a downtown New York nightclub with a rock star friend of his. Can you imagine the headlines if she'd stayed with him?

Ivanka didn't tell me much about her dating life between the cocky guy and Jared. I heard rumors about athletes and movie stars, but I didn't intrude or ask for the details. She was a grown woman. If she wanted to talk to me about her boyfriends, I was always there for her, but she preferred to keep her personal life to herself. At one point, Donald wanted her to date Tom Brady, the quarterback. He said, "You have to meet him!" But Ivanka wasn't into it.

When she was twenty-six, she was set up with Jared Kushner by mutual friends. He came from a New York real estate family and was—is—a wealthy businessman in his own right and the owner of the *New York Observer*. I met him at a dinner of just the three of us and I liked him immediately. He was intelligent and good-looking, and they obviously adored each other. I assumed they'd take the next step, but Ivanka told me, "His family won't let him marry me because I'm not Jewish."

I asked, "What are you going to do?"

She was torn about it, and she broke up with him. But they

really loved each other and got back together a year later. The core problem hadn't changed, though. I told her, "I don't care about religion. You were born Catholic and your roots won't change. But if he makes you happy, go for it." She converted, and they got married in 2009 at the Trump National Golf Club in Bedminster, New Jersey.

IVANKA

As a wedding present, one of our friends gave us a five-night stay at a gorgeous hotel that he owned in Italy. We were so excited to finally be able to take the trip, almost a year later. On the first day we arrived in Sardinia, I got a text from my mother that said she was on a friend's boat in the area and heard we were in town so they were "dropping anchor." She was coming ashore and had booked a room in the same hotel so we could catch up. My mother crashed our romantic getaway! We spent the days with her, and she did her own thing at night. She hardly ever ate with us because dinner at nine p.m. was like a second lunch for her. When her night was just getting started, we'd be in bed.

Ivanka and Jared are incredibly happy, which is all I care about. They've been married for eight years and have three children. He's a great father, and they're still crazy about each other. Jared is strong. If he doesn't agree with something she's said or done, he tells her right away. It takes real guts to put my daughter in her place, right in front of his mother-in-law—and I'm not your typical mother-in-law. He's either very comfortable around me, or they're comfortable being complimentary *and* critical of each other, or all of the above.

And now I have a Jewish daughter and grandchildren. Eighty-five percent of my friends, including my best friend, Nikki Haskell, are Jewish. However, most of my friends are not observant, hardly ever go to temple, and don't keep kosher. None of them are Orthodox, which the Kushners are. When they used to visit me in Palm Beach on the weekend, they'd walk from the synagogue to Concha Marina to have tea and cookies. *Walk!* For miles in scorching heat in their nice clothes. They had to be exhausted and I always offered to have my driver take them home. But, according to custom, they couldn't ride in a car on the Sabbath. So they walked back to Mar-a-Lago.

In New York, when Ivanka and I get manicures together at Nail Niche on a Saturday, she can't touch money, so I pay (I would pay anyway). One Saturday, the doorbell rang unexpectedly. It was Ivanka with her two oldest kids. She said, "Mom, get dressed and come with us now. And bring cash!"

I said, "Why? Where are we going?"

It turned out that her friend Wendi Deng, the former wife of Rupert Murdoch, and her two daughters, Chloe and Grace, were selling cupcakes on Fifth Avenue to raise funds for a new locker room at their school. It was the Sabbath, so Ivanka couldn't purchase a freaking cupcake! They were one dollar apiece, with only five left. I offered them the four singles I had on me for all five cupcakes, but they wouldn't budge. Then a friend of mine walked by—actually, the aunt of Ivanka's cocky ex-boyfriend—and I said,

"Do you want to buy a cupcake for a dollar?" She did, and we gave the Murdoch girls the money. Then we stood on Fifth Avenue in a small circle—Ivanka, her children, my friend, and I—and ate Wendi Deng's cupcakes. It was a sweet moment, one we wouldn't have had if Ivanka could carry her wallet on Saturday.

Eric was the last one to get married. He was barely out of college when he met Lara Yunaska, a sporty pastry chef and dog person. What's not to love? When they met, she was a TV producer at *Inside Edition*. She runs five miles a day and loves horseback riding. Eric and Lara didn't rush into anything; they dated for six years before getting engaged. She's a very nice girl, intelligent, hardworking, all the things I admire in a person.

I threw Lara a bridal shower at my house for family, including Ivanka, and her many friends. It was a classic shower with pastries, drinks, and presents. I hired a piano player to entertain us, and we did the ritual of her opening her gifts. She got lingerie (of course), perfumes, candles, some jewelry, chocolates. Eric stopped by at the end, and we got to raise our glasses to toast them together.

They got married at (guess where?) Mar-a-Lago in 2014. Two weeks before the wedding, she had a horseback riding accident and broke one of her wrists. I worry about Lara and her riding. Last year, she fell again and broke her collarbone. I told Eric, "She keeps getting hurt. Maybe she should stop." (I don't think she'll be riding much these days, since she's pregnant with their first child. I'm already planning her baby shower!) She might just be accident-prone, and it may be spreading to Eric, too. She took him on a jog once and he came back with a twisted ankle. He was on crutches for months. Anyway, on her wedding day, she wore satin sleeves over her arms to hide the cast as she walked down the aisle. They didn't cover her fingers, so her diamond engagement ring—from Ivanka's collection—flashed in the lights. Their miniature beagle Charlie was the ring bearer, and Jared officiated. (For the record, it was not a Jewish ceremony, as was reported in many media outlets.) I walked down the aisle with Eric and sat next to Donald, Melania, and Barron at the ceremony, which was okay. At the dinner, I sat with Dorothy and Babi, which was better.

At that wedding, Donald and I did share a moment of gratitude for the family we created together. All of our children are married, and once Eric's son arrives, we'll have nine grandchildren. Six boys and three girls! (We need more girls.) Donald and I started the whole thing and have watched our family grow, and grow, and grow! Nine little monsters! It's so many freaking Trumps. I love it . . . and I'm getting scared!

PRIDE OF THE LION GLAM-MA

My best advice to Ivanka, Vanessa, and Lara about what I learned from my own three pregnancies is to take it easy on yourself (which I never did, but should have), don't wear high heels (which I did until the eighth month), and watch your diet. Ivanka only gained twenty-five pounds for each of her pregnancies. After she had Theodore last March, she was back at work in two days (just like me) and was down to her pre-pregnancy weight by the time she spoke at the Republican convention just a few months later, and looked fabulous.

Don and Vanessa welcomed Kai, my first grandchild, to the world in May 2007. At the hospital, I congratulated the new parents and said, "Welcome to the club." I warned each one that from this point on, no matter what they did or where they went, part of them would be thinking about the health and happiness of this tiny creature. Don put Kai in my arms and I gave her a hug and a kiss. "Yup, she's a baby!" I said. I held her for a few minutes, and then I got bored and gave her back. Newborn babies aren't that interesting to me anymore, I must confess. They're a lot more fun when they're five or six and can hold up their end of a conversation. Kai is now nine, and she loves to dance and perform. She's got a big personality, just like me. Donald III (Donnie), eight, is a very sweet boy. He reminds me of Don, actually. Tristan, five, is a little troublemaker! He jumps around from sofa to sofa, and I run after him making sure he doesn't hit his head. He needs to be watched constantly. Recently, he broke his leg on a skiing trip in Aspen and had to get a full leg cast, poor boy. What I do to quiet the little hell-raiser is give him a project, like drawing with special fabric crayons and Mickey Mouse stencils on T-shirts. That one kept him busy for hours. Spencer, four, is following after his older brothers, like Eric did with Don. He's already very bright. Chloe, two, is a beautiful angel baby with a round face and enormous blue eyes. She's absolutely gorgeous.

After Ivanka had Arabella in July 2011, she called me and said, "Mom, I'm a mom." I rushed to the hospital to meet my newest grandchild. Hug, hug, kiss, kiss, snap, snap. And then I left so Ivanka could get some much-deserved rest. I came to the hospital to meet Joseph in October 2013 and Theodore in March 2016. I'm not the type to go in the delivery room and hold her hand. I don't think anyone should be in the room except for the mother and her doctor, and definitely not the father! As I said earlier, a man sees a baby come out, and your sex life will go down the tubes. Arabella, six, is a little show-off. She comes over after her ballet lessons, in pink tights and a bodysuit, and sings and dances for me. Just like her mom, she loves *The Sound of Music* and can belt out all the songs. Last April, Arabella, then five, serenaded Chinese president Xi Jinping and Madame Peng Liyuan at a state visit while her brother Joseph, a sweet, shy boy, hid in his father's jacket. Her song was in Chinese. Arabella's nanny is from China and is teaching her the language.

Both Vanessa and Ivanka were breastfeeders. It wasn't for me, but if a mother wants to attach a baby to her boob, do one side, then the other side, burp him, get him to take a nap, and then do it all over again when he wakes up, go right ahead. For me, it just wasn't possible. I was working ten-hour days and needed to sleep for longer than three hours at a stretch. I have no regrets about bottle-feeding my kids. They were all strong and intelligent, they never got sick, and they all grew to be six feet tall. Whatever you choose, it's fine. What matters is that you are at peace with the decision. A stressed-out mom is going to have stressed-out kids. I also had a lot of support. If it weren't for Trudy, Bridget, and Dorothy, there was no way I could have accomplished so much in my career, on the charity circuit, or as a coordinator of the kids' activities and educations. Working mothers back then and nowadays need help! Ivanka is doing her all to make life easier for families with legislation about child-care tax credits and generous family leave. I know she's going to do a lot of good for millions of people.

Vanessa and Ivanka are both excellent mothers, as I'm sure Lara will be, too. Vanessa is very strict. She takes no nonsense. If one of her kids jumps on the coffee table, she corrects him immediately. I've never had to bite my lip about either Ivanka's or Vanessa's parenting choices—because they are always what I would do myself. Even if I did have criticism, I would keep it to myself. It's not my job to give advice unless I'm really disturbed by something. Parents have their own way of doing things, and as long as the children are happy and healthy and the family is together, whatever strategies and techniques they use are okay with me. Every kid is different, and responds to different motivations and punishments.

—————————— IVANKA ——————————

When I had kids of my own, it definitely made me see my mother in a different way. I now recognize how difficult it is to parent well.

It's not fun to punish your kids, and it's often at your own expense. I have had full Sundays ruined having to cancel family outings that we were all excited about in favor of grounding Arabella or Joseph for misbehaving. It'd be easier, and frankly more fun, to just ignore the bad behavior, but you can't, even if you really want to. It's particularly hard to say no when you're exhausted. I'll come home from work on some days, and I'm so tired, all I want to do is play and cuddle with the kids.

I'm not crazy about Vanessa's workload with five kids. How much quality time can she or any woman spend with each kid each day? Three was hard enough. I can't image how she does it with five.

She's juggling all of their schedules, schools, activities, constantly picking up one or the other from this place or that place. If Don and Vanessa said they were having another kid, I'd be shocked. During the campaign, when Don was traveling constantly for eighteen months to support his father, Vanessa dealt with her huge family by herself. Even with help from nannies, it's still five bedtime stories, five baths, five homework hours. She doesn't get a break until ten p.m.! Only a woman could deal with it. A man would crumble with half the workload.

I help out when I can, too. Every week I'm in New York, the kids come to my house, or I go to theirs, at four p.m., the crazy hour. The grandkids call me Glam-Ma or Ivana-Ma. We play, sing and dance, make cookies and candles. I was very strict about giving candy to my children. We didn't allow sweets in the house. I found out later that whenever my parents came to visit, they would bring a suitcase full of Czech candy for Don, Ivanka, and Eric. Well, now it's my turn. As a Glam-Ma, it's my job to spoil my grandchildren, so I give them as much candy and cake as they can eat! Then, after two hours or whenever I've had enough, I pass them back to their moms.

IVANKA

All the tough-love stuff that she applied to us growing up? She either intentionally ignores the rules or has forgotten all about them at this phase of her life. She indulges my kids completely. There is a direct correlation between my kids' every stomachache and spending time at Glam-Ma's house. She takes Arabella to get manicures as a special treat, which is a highlight for them both. She buys them

T-shirts from all her travels. If you ask my kids if they want to go to Glam-Ma's, they always say, "Yes!" I think a big draw was Tiger, Mom's dog. He was like her fourth child. My kids loved hanging out with him. I'm not sure how Tiger felt about it. They tortured him by relentlessly chasing him around.

Last spring, I did something I've never done before: attended a bris. Catholic boys are circumcised in the hospital right after birth. Theodore was done when he was eight days old at Jared's parents' house by a mohel in front of family and guests. There were prayers first, and the poor kid was crying the whole time. I respect the custom, as uncomfortable as it was to watch. Look, it is what it is. Ivanka and Jared are raising their children in their faith. I applaud them for it, but I far prefer going to the kids' regular birthday parties.

I'm back on the recitals/school plays/soccer games circuit. Not only do the kids' schools have Parents' Day, they also have Grandparents' Day. Compared to the other grandparents, who are in wheelchairs, I feel like a high school freshman. *I don't belong in the room!* I think, looking around at the gray-haired biddies and doddering grandpas. In a few cases, I'm not much older than my grandchildren's classmates' fathers.

───────────────── DON ─────────────────

When Mom is in town, she comes to Grandparents' Day at my kids' school, and there have been many of them! I remember one in particular, where Donnie and Glam-Ma were doing some coloring at a kids' table. My mother was sitting in one of the little chairs, getting really into her drawing, becoming a kid again before our eyes . . . and the leader of the pack of all the other kids in the class, who were clamoring to sit next to her!

Seeing the decrepit crowd at Grandparents' Day is a little depressing, to tell you the truth. I feel so much younger than my contemporaries look. (Maybe this is why I'm attracted to men in their thirties and forties. We're the same age when it comes to energy.) I felt the same way when I went to a college reunion in Prague and saw that so many of my classmates looked withered or bloated, sometimes both! Many of them seemed not to care if they lived or died. They had no reason to get out of bed every day.

No one can stop time, but aging is a choice you make. I choose to slow the process by eating well, sleeping well, and taking care of myself. I hit the exercise room every morning. Every year, I go skiing in Aspen in December, to St. Moritz in February, and sometimes back to Aspen in April. I frolic in the South of France with young men. I read three papers each morning and book after book, and watch all the TV news. I know what's going on in the world and am still firmly in control of my businesses and investments. With so much going on, as well as a soccer team's worth of grandchildren to keep me on my toes, I'm way too busy to give up on life! Nothing is going to slow me down until I'm dead. Maybe not even then.

• • •

Family holidays with all the kids are a logistical nightmare. These days, it's practically impossible, especially with the Secret Service protecting them. (Speaking as a mother and grandmother, I'm very glad that they are.) Don's family consists of seven people. Ivanka's is five. Eric and Lara will be three. We have four dogs among us. Counting Babi and me, we'd need a house with fourteen bedrooms to get all of us under one roof.

Mar-a-Lago is certainly large enough, but the problem (for me anyway) is that it's Donald and Melania's house. Although I'm welcome there, it's a bit weird to hang out at my ex's mansion with his third wife, their son, and her parents. My mother does it all the time, though, so she can be near her grandchildren and great-grandchildren. She doesn't find it strange in the least for the mother of the first wife to live under the same roof as the third wife.

I do show up for certain holidays, though, or I'd never get to see all my children in one place. Last Easter, I went to Mar-a-Lago for the day. I have a Mini Cooper for running around in Miami. Palm Beach is only seventy-three miles away, so I decided to drive down for the day. Everything was fine until the gas light went on.

I pulled over at a highway service area with a McDonald's and a Shell station, and pulled up to a gas pump. A sign said SELF-SERVICE. I had no freaking clue what to do. I got out, picked up the hose, and opened the little door for the gas tank, but I couldn't get the gas to start flowing. I was standing there, squeezing the pump, looking like a fool.

A young guy got out of his weathered Ford pickup next to me, and I said, "Excuse me, can you help me fill up my car, please?"

He said, "Of course, Ivana. I'll help you. Give me your credit card."

I gave him my card and he did the necessary button pushing to unlock the gas. Success! I filled the tank.

"You have to go inside the store to get your receipt," he said.

That was a disaster, because I forgot to read which pump was mine. The man helped me with that, too. When the ordeal was over, I gave him $100 and said, "Buy yourself a pizza and some wine, and please tell me how to get to I-95 North!"

Back on the highway, I felt excellent about the full tank of gas and made it to Palm Beach in no time. We had a barbecue lunch by the pool. All the grandkids were swimming and running around. Vanessa was chasing after them as always. Don, Eric, and Donald left to play golf. My mother, Ivanka, Lara, Vanessa, Donald's sisters, and I sat together chatting for a while.

I left after lunch and drove south, got turned around by the Miami airport, somehow got lost, and ended up in Brickell, a downtown Miami neighborhood. I saw a police car and asked, "How do I get to South Beach?"

"Okay, Ivana, this is what you're going to do . . ." the officer said, and gave a series of directions I forgot two seconds later.

Half an hour passed, and I was still driving in circles. A woman in a convertible pulled up next to me and I yelled, "Excuse me! Can you help me get to South Beach?"

She said, "Sure, Ivana. Just follow me!" She led me to the right exit and I made it home.

Later that night, my phone rang. It was an Italian friend of mine, who said, "Were you in Brickell in a Mini Cooper today at five p.m.?"

Huh? How did he know that? "Yes."

"The woman in the convertible? That was my wife!"

Miami: just as small a town as New York City. I calculated later that I'd spent as much time in the car driving around lost as I did having quality time with my family! Next time, I'm taking an Uber.

MY WORK HERE IS (ALMOST) DONE

When Donald and I were married, we went to the US Open tennis tournament in Flushing Meadows, Queens, every September. We had a six-seat box right by the courts, and I rooted for Czech players Ivan Lendl and Martina Navratilova, or whichever player, regardless of country, was winning. Winning was everything. Donald later upgraded to a bigger box right next to the commentators, with butlers and a buffet, big enough to seat fifteen. Sometimes, the kids would come. Often, he gave tickets to employees.

One time in our early years, Donald and I went to a big finals match and couldn't find the driver to our limo outside the stadium. Donald said, "Let's take the subway. I know Queens really well."

We walked with the crowd to the subway platform. We boarded the train and a reporter jumped into the car with us just as the doors were closing. The ride between Queens and Manhattan was only about fifteen minutes. The whole time, the reporter took pictures of us. What could we do? There was nowhere to hide, so we just allowed it and laughed it off.

The next day, the *New York Post* ran a cover of us on the subway with the headline, "Donald and Ivana Are Just Like Us!"

I tell this story now, at the end of my book, because writing it has brought to mind all the things I, as a mother, have in common with every parent: dreams of a healthy, happy life for my children, the hope that they'll achieve something great, the desire to maintain close family bonds. My children feel the same way about their own. The Trumps really are just like everyone else in many ways.

Then again, we're obviously *not* a typical American family—or even a typical wealthy, privileged American family. The Trumps are a breed of their own. I've been asking myself what makes us different while writing this book. What qualities set my kids apart? Why are they so often misunderstood or misinterpreted?

It comes down to three things: unbridled confidence, boundless energy, and fierce determination. My children have been raised to have drive, a hatred for losing, and the stamina to keep pushing until they ultimately win.

At the same debate where Hillary Clinton raved about my children, Donald gave her a compliment, too. He said, "She doesn't quit. She doesn't give up. I respect that. She's a fighter. I disagree with much of what she's fighting for . . . but she doesn't give up, and I consider that to be a very good trait." He appreciated that quality in her because it's mirrored in himself, and in his children. What attracted Donald to me all those years ago at Maxwell's Plum was my energy. I vibrated on a higher level than everyone else, and he could see it. What attracted me to him was his confidence. Together, we made three children who have the best of both of us. And, as I've always said, if you can't be the best, don't bother.

With love, I raised them to be tough. Don's, Ivanka's, and Eric's determination was founded in the lessons I taught them, but life circumstances forced them to be strong and resilient. The divorce. The deaths. Living away from home. Emotional turmoil. Some social isolation. Intense pressure to succeed. Living in a public eye that never blinks. Relentless and brutal mockery and ridicule in the media. It's not going to stop, either.

The campaign and election were stressful and demanding, and for those long eighteen months, the kids were busy with their father, living on airplanes, going to three cities in a day to meet thousands of people at rallies and events. Meanwhile, their spouses and families were left behind. I didn't see them that often, either, in 2016. I hoped to spend some time with them during the inauguration weekend, but I had to cut that short and get my mother back home to New York. She needed a few days to relax at my town house before the trip back to Prague for the rest of the winter. Who knows if we'll ever see her again? She's ninety-two. It's her choice to go back and forth between the Czech Republic and America. I can't stop her, but I do worry about her when we're apart.

The kids feel the same way I do about Babi. They're all very close with her. When she's in town, she goes with Don and his family to their country house every weekend, and visits Eric and Lara at their house. After Ivanka moved to Washington, Babi saw her less, but she'd previously gone to the Kushners' home in New Jersey and to Ivanka's retreat in Bedminster. Babi adores her great-grandchildren and helps take care of them, just like she helped me take care of my kids. During the handful of days between the inauguration and Babi's return to Prague, all three of the kids came to East Sixty-Fourth Street one by one to have tea, say good-bye, and chat about the future as members of the First Family.

Eric arrived early. He'd only just learned that Lara was pregnant and we talked about the possibility of his moving to a bigger apartment. FYI: all my kids bought their apartments in New York in Trump buildings with their own money. When Donald gets mad, he says, "Get out of my house!" By using their own money, the kids didn't have to deal with that.

While we talked, I felt proud of the man Eric's become. He's sweet and strong, very focused and hardworking. I have no doubt that he'll continue to do well in the Trump Organization and figure out where to go with it next, beyond golf courses and the winery. He's confident in himself, knows who he is, what he wants to do. He's come a long way from the boy I had to remind to sit up straight in TV interviews. There's not a journalist's question in the world that can knock him off his line, and I can see him doing more and more press as time goes on. Even though he's the youngest, he's not the weakest. His big brother used to look after him. His big sister used to take care of him like he was her own little bambino. He doesn't need their help anymore. He's grown up to be confident and capable, and he's doing fantastically well.

Don came next. We talked about the Trump Organization with him, too, and what was going to happen now that Donald and Ivanka were out. No one knows exactly what to expect, and there is some confusion. Don was working hard to smooth over any uncertainty and grow the company. The boys have plenty of work to do just maintaining the existing properties, but they intend to build new ones, too.

Meanwhile, he's got five children under ten and an international company to run. When he gets home, the kids are running around, yelling and screaming. I worry about Don and Vanessa's kids at their schools, and the possibility of the other students giving them a hard time. It's a lot to deal with, but he has a real talent for being able to let it all go on the weekends. He takes his family to their cottage in the Catskills for fishing and driving around on ATVs. He really needs his family time to unwind.

Of all the kids, Don took the hardest hits during the campaign and continues to do so. Everything the kids do is being watched and criticized. Eric and Ivanka ignore the jabs from the press. As Eric says, "You have to pick your battles. I think you have to realize that many things don't matter, and if you're offended by every little thing, you're going to live a pretty tough life." Don worries me because he has the softest heart. When the media goes after his siblings, he's more outraged on their behalf than they are. But he's getting better at letting it roll off his back.

Ivanka came last. She talked about her new house in Kalorama, her plans for the kids, and what she hoped to accomplish. Since that day, she's been given an official job with security clearance. I worry about how she's going to do it all: be a mother, wife, and White House staffer; adjust to her new house, new city, and new schools for the kids; and take care of herself, too. My mother is too diplomatic to say something to Ivanka, but behind closed doors, she told me she's concerned, too. My daughter is thirty-five and has set her mind on this. What Ivanka wants, Ivanka gets. She's very smart and has always made wise decisions, none wiser than marrying Jared. I think he's fabulous. I'm not convinced about some of the Orthodox customs, but if Ivanka was willing to give up lobster and bacon, she must really love him.

Maybe in fifteen years, she could run for president. Who knows? I think it could happen for Jared or Ivanka. We'll see how they feel after living in Washington for four years. Whatever Ivanka wants to do is fine with me. If she feels strongly about working for change, she'll do well. She's intelligent and has been trained to fight hard and face any challenge.

First Lady? Holds no appeal for me personally.

First Mother? That could work.

Nowadays, I just stand back and watch my kids go. I don't interfere or give them advice. And if I did, I'm not sure they'd take it! But I'd try to remind them of the most important lessons I've lived by and learned the hard way myself:

1. **Surround yourself with loyal people.** If you can't trust those closest to you, you might as well be alone.

2. **Make a name for yourself.** With Trump as a last name, they carry the burden of other people's assumptions. That said, they can differentiate themselves with their first names. I'm known as Ivana. My businesses are named

Ivana. Eric has put his name on his charitable foundation, and he's become known for that. Ivanka put her name on her brands. It's a winning strategy.

3. **Set goals.** I'm sixty-eight, and at a stage in my life where I'm happy to enjoy the fruits of my labors. I can relax now because I have been a goal setter all along, and I've achieved every one I set my sights on, or got as close as I possibly could. I hope the kids continue to set goals and work to achieve them in whatever they do in life.

4. **Ignore the noise.** Why pay so much attention or cry a single tear over the opinions of people who don't even know you? There's simply no point.

5. **No regrets.** I have only one: In the eighties, Andy Warhol wanted to paint my portrait. Donald said no, so we didn't do it. It'd be worth a ton by now! Other than not doing that, I regret nothing. I keep my eyes on the future, never look back, and can't wait to see what happens next.

—Ivana Trump, New York City, June 1, 2017

ACKNOWLEDGMENTS

Telling your life story takes a lot of work and requires a lot of help. I'd like to thank all the people who were instrumental in the creation of *Raising Trump*.

First, I want to thank my children, Don Jr., Ivanka, and Eric, for contributing their stories throughout these pages. My book about your childhoods is all the more special to me because we did it together.

To Vanessa, Jared, and Lara and all of my fabulous grandchildren for making my children's lives full and happy, and for bringing so much joy into my life, too.

Donald, my ex-husband, has been a friend for so many years. Thanks for supporting me in everything I've done and for a lot of happy memories and good times.

My mother, Marie, aka Babi, remembers everything, and she reminded me of a few stories I'd forgotten. Thanks for all you've done for me, including your help with this book.

Dorothy Curry, my personal assistant, spent weeks going through thousands of photographs, as well as researching dates, mining her memories, and supporting me throughout the writing of the book. I'm grateful, as always, for all you do.

Thanks to my friends, especially Nikki Haskell, who has been my friend for years and has photographed me and my family forever; my dear friend Vivian Serota, who has been a great support to me for a long time; and my dear friend Massimo Gargia, for his friendship over forty years. Two of my best friends are my ex-husbands Riccardo Mazzucchelli and Rossano Rubicondi. Thank you both for being in my life and for all the fun we've had.

Eva, my assistant in Europe, makes my life possible. Thanks!

Daniel Strone, my agent, has been my champion at every step of the publishing process. Thank you for your guidance and belief in the project. Also, my thanks to Katie in Dan's office for her invaluable support.

The team at Gallery Books has been amazing from our earliest conversations—and later our three-hour lunches. My thanks to all of you, for Jennifer Bergstrom's grand vision, Nina Cordes's keen eye for details, Carolyn Reidy's commitment, Jennifer Robinson's great instincts, and Elisa Rivlin's excellent judgment.

Gary Lyman, my lawyer, has been in my life forever, and he contributed to this book as an early reader and sounding board. Thanks again for your humor, intelligence, and wise advice.

To Tiger, my beloved constant companion of eleven years, who died suddenly, devastatingly during the writing of this book. And to Tiger 2, my new doggie friend, who is just finding his feet in our family and already winning hearts.

Finally, Valerie Frankel has been a pleasure to work with from day one. The strength and ease of our collaboration is evident on every page. Thanks, Val, for accommodating my crazy schedule and making hard work so much fun.